Watching the Moon
and
Other Plays

Luigi Pirandello and Massimo Bontempelli in Buenos Aires, 1933.

Watching the Moon
and
Other Plays
by
Massimo Bontempelli

Translation and Introduction
by
Patricia Gaborik

Italica Press
New York
2013

Copyright © 2013 by Patricia Gaborik
ITALICA PRESS RENAISSANCE AND MODERN PLAYS SERIES
ITALICA PRESS, INC.
595 MAIN STREET
NEW YORK, NEW YORK 10044

All rights reserved. No part of this publication may be reproduced, stored in a retrieval system, or transmitted, in any form or by any means, electronic, mechanical, photocopying, recording, or otherwise, without prior permission of Italica Press. For permission to reproduce selected portions for courses, please contact the Press at
inquiries@italicapress.com.

LIBRARY OF CONGRESS CATALOGING-IN-PUBLICATION DATA
Bontempelli, Massimo, 1878–1960.
[Plays. Selections]
Watching the Moon and Other Plays / by Massimo Bontempelli ; Translation and Introduction by Patricia Gaborik.
   pages cm. -- (Italica Press Renaissance and Modern Plays Series)
Includes bibliographical references.
Summary: "Presents the first English translations of three plays by the important Futurist poet, playwright, novelist and composer, Massimo Bontempelli, including "Watching the Moon" (La guardia alla luna, 1916), "Stormcloud" (Nembo, 1935) and "Cinderella" (1942), with an extensive introduction on the author and his work"-- Provided by publisher.
   ISBN 978-1-59910-279-5 (Hardcover : alk. paper) -- ISBN 978-1-59910-280-1 (Paperback : alk. paper) -- ISBN 978-1-59910-281-8 (E-Book)
 I. Gaborik, Patricia. II. Title.
 PQ4807.O65A6 2013
 852'.912--dc23
                                                          2013029921

Cover art: Photo graphics by Anna T. Ambrosini

FOR A COMPLETE LIST OF TITLES IN
RENAISSANCE AND MODERN PLAYS
VISIT OUR WEB SITE AT
WWW.ITALICAPRESS.COM

Contents

About the Translator	vi
Acknowledgements	vii
Introduction	ix
A Note on the Translations	lxv
Further Reading	lxix
Watching the Moon	1
Stormcloud	31
Cinderella	67

About the Translator

Patricia Gaborik is an independent scholar and playwright based in Italy. A fellow of the American Academy in Rome, she holds doctoral degrees in Theatre History Studies from the University of Wisconsin and the University of Rome, "La Sapienza." She has published in various collections, such journals as *Modern Drama, Theatre Survey, Western European Stages* and *Dance Research Journal*, and is now completing a monograph on theater in Mussolini's Italy.

Acknowledgements

Chief among the institutions deserving my thanks for this volume is the American Academy in Rome, where, in 2005–6 as a Post-doctoral Fellow in Modern Italian Studies, I carried on the research of my dissertation years — on Massimo Bontempelli's theater — and these translations, then just begun, as a Paul Mellon Postdoctoral Fellow. The American Society for Theatre Research, the University of Wisconsin Graduate Student Council and Department of Theatre and Drama, and the Getty Research Institute all gave travel funds, making possible archival research both in Italy and in the US. The Getty Research Institute Special Collections hosts the Massimo Bontempelli papers, crucial to the completion of this project and source of the many newspaper clippings, letters and photographic materials cited or otherwise used here. Wim de Wit and the Special Collections staff at the Getty, the staffs at the Fondazione Primo Conti and the Archivio Centrale dello Stato, and Paola Pettenella of the MART (Museo d'Arte Moderna e Contemporaneo di Trento e Rovereto), I must thank for the kind assistance in tracking down materials. Alvise Memmo deserves special gratitude not only for agreeing to the publication of these texts, but for his friendly, enthusiastic conversation about Bontempelli and my work over the years.

In ways big and small, several colleagues and friends have helped this publication see the light of day. First among these is Edward Muir, who set me down the path of Italian studies. Next came those professors who oversaw — officially or otherwise — my first Bontempellian explorations during graduate school: Jon Snyder, Lucia Re, Patrick Rumble, Michael Peterson, Aparna Dharwadker and especially Mike Vanden Heuvel and Marc Silberman. Since, invitations by Patty Gallagher, Paulo Lemos Horta and Pierpaolo Antonello to speak, respectively, at UC Santa Cruz, NYU Abu Dhabi and Cambridge University gave me further opportunities to think through the issues discussed and plays presented here. Gaby Ford and the actors of the English Theatre of Rome kindly organized a reading, simply so that I could hear the texts spoken aloud by voices other than my own. I am ever grateful for sustained, stimulating and enjoyable conversation about Bontempelli, the avant-garde and fascist culture with Emilio Gentile, Kimberly

Acknowledgements

Jannarone and Luca Somigli. Andrea Harris deserves special recognition for her smart and attentive reading, not only of the introductory essay here, but of countless pages over the years. My heartiest and affectionate appreciation go to Ernesto Livorni, who in the very early days talked about the shape this book should have and worked with me on the translation, especially of *La guardia alla luna*.

Finally, it is with all my love and gratitude that I dedicate this volume to Gabriele Pedullà, perhaps the only other being on earth who thinks of Bontempelli every time he crosses a Roman street to get out of the sun and into the shade.

Introduction

Massimo Bontempelli: The King of Chameleons?

Massimo Bontempelli was born under the sign of speed. It was May 12, 1878 when he came into the world, and life was beginning to move pretty fast: ships cruised the oceans, bikes and trains sped by, steam trams were under operation and soon electric ones would be, too. If automobiles weren't yet fully revved — the first US car race saw its winner travel from Green Bay to Madison, Wisconsin in just over thirty-three hours (about six mph) — the Transcontinental Express had wowed everyone, reaching San Francisco from New York in eighty-three hours, thirty-nine minutes. Phileas Fogg and Passepartout had indeed already shown that by ship and train you could venture *Around the World in Eighty Days* (Jules Verne's novel had debuted five years before).

Young Massimo's father Alfonso was a railroad engineer and for that work moved frequently, taking the boy and his mother, Maria Cislaghi, everywhere he went. From Como to Milan to Codogna they would go; back to Milan and on to Mortara, Chiavari Civitavecchia; to Milan once again and then to Voghera and Alessandria, all before Massimo completed high school. A passion for geography, for travel and the means of it — for trams, trains and automobiles — would lace the writer's entire oeuvre, which includes poetry, fiction, plays and journalistic writings (not to mention musical compositions). A sampling of book and chapter titles alone attests to the central role that voyaging holds in his work: "The Man with the Big Suitcase," "From Home to the Station," "Railway Dawn," *Adventures by Land and Sea* ("Signore con valigia grande," "Da casa alla stazione," "Alba ferroviaria," *Avventure di terra e di mare*). Who's to say that Massimo Bontempelli's fascination with iron rails and their metallic steeds, his delight in riding the trams that collapsed the distance between Milanese squares, his desire to speed around "countries made above all of roads"[1] weren't instilled by his first experiences as son of the railroad engineer who studied train routes and timetables, who took the lad to the yard to see those massive locomotives, who could boast

---

1. Massimo Bontempelli, *Pezzi di mondo* (Milano: Panorama Casa Editrice Italiana, 1936), 140. Unless otherwise noted, all translations are mine.

Introduction

of designing those iron pathways that ripped across the industrious and industrializing Italian north like no mere motor car could?

It's easy to imagine the thrill — and trepidation — a young Massimo felt each time he climbed aboard the hulking train, which would wait for him as he bid farewell to the friends he had made in one city, before speeding him off to the next and into his future, where he would begin the wonderful-terrible cycle all over again. That Bontempelli's paeans to the motorized world carried with them ironic and melancholy reflections, too, is hardly surprising: this was, as Stephen Kern so eloquently dubbed it, "the culture of time and space," where a "revolution of the broadest scope was taking place, one that involved essential structures of human experience and basic forms of human expression."[2] Bontempelli's experience would find beautifully unique expression over several phases in a nearly six-decade career; it's not just the vehicles cruising his landscape that recall his childhood, but the repeated farewells that such a vagabond youth would have entailed — for the course of the author's intellectual life would be marked by a series of clamorous goodbyes. These adieus were utter repudiations: the discarding of once-favored literary styles and techniques, political creeds and single works representative of these. Each disavowal was the first step of a new trek to the frontier of Italian letters, for when Bontempelli embarked on a new adventure, he never just slipped quietly out the door. No! He slammed it furiously, set his shoulders square and strode off down the walk.

The railroad engineer's son was as fascinated by the classical world as he was by the mechanized one that would spring up around him as the twentieth century progressed, and it's thus with good reason he's been called a "polyhedral" writer — not only did he go through many phases, but his interests were always multi-faceted and surprising.[3] Many of his first publications — *Egloghe, Verseggiando, Odi siciliane* (*Eclogues, Versifying, Sicilian Odes*) —

---

2. Stephen Kern, *The Culture of Time and Space, 1880–1918* (Cambridge, MA: Harvard University Press, 1983), 6.
3. In his introduction to an indispensable issue of *L'Illuminista* entirely dedicated to Bontempelli, Walter Pedullà writes, "Polyhedral writer, Bontempelli must be sought with every means and method." "Dovuto a Bontempelli," *L'Illuminista* 5.13–15 (January–December 2005): 14. The expression is particularly apt when one considers that the climactic third act of Bontempelli's *Nostra Dea* takes place in what he named the "polyhedric palace."

Introduction

were poetic volumes, of a classicism in the vein of renowned Nobel Laureate Giosue Carducci.[4] After several years of teaching in various provinces, which inspired his first short story collection, *Socrate moderno (Modern Socrates*, 1908), the author abandoned that career and moved to Florence, where he edited such journals as *Cronache letterarie* (1910–12) and *Acropoli* (1911), founded by famed scholar and translator of ancient Greek literature Ettore Romangnoli.

Then World War I came. Bontempelli had clamored for Italy's participation in the conflict, was a correspondent from the front and went to the trenches in 1917, where he served as an artillery officer. During the war, he became friends with a number of those writers and artists who had launched the literary and art movement futurism in 1909, especially Carlo Carrà. These encounters would change everything. In 1915 Bontempelli had chosen not to release his play *La doppia vita* (*The Double Life*) because he felt that people went to the theater only for distraction. Instead, what both the public and the new authors should feel was "one duty and one desire: action."[5] But under futurist influence, he would quickly become convinced that art — literature, theater — were crucial to the practice of politics and social change. They were, as he would later write, the attempt to overcome the contrast between contemplation and action: the tools for combating an increasingly materialist and superficial bourgeois society.[6]

This was his conversion to the avant-garde, where being avant-garde didn't just mean experimenting with form and style, but instigating social, political and cultural change through works of art. The 1916 *La guardia alla luna*, in this volume translated as *Watching the Moon*, is an exploration of what such a conversion

---

4. Giosuè Carducci (1835–1907) was so revered by Italians as to be considered a sort of national poet; he was also the country's first recipient of the Nobel Prize in Literature. Though a great classicist poet, he was also a bold experimenter with poetic meter.
5. From an article in the *Giornale d'Italia*, November 1915, retrieved in the Getty Research Institute Special Collections, Massimo Bontempelli papers, hereafter abbreviated as GRI, followed by the box number and, if available, folder number. GRI 62.
6. September of 1934, in Bontempelli, *L'avventura novecentista: Selva polemica (1926–1938)*, (Firenze: Vallecchi, 1938), 306, a volume gathering various writings from 1926–38, hereafter abbreviated as *AN*. The most readily available version of *AN* dates to 1974 (Firenze: Vallecchi); this edition, by Ruggero Jacobbi, is, however, trimmed of its politically compromising passages.

Introduction

would mean in stylistic terms: previously he had written *Costanza* (*Constance*, 1905), a patriotic verse tragedy modeled on those by the revered Italian poet Gabriele D'Annunzio, who later become a national hero for his military exploits, and two naturalist pieces — *La Piccola* and *Santa Teresa* (*The Little One* and *Saint Teresa*, 1915) — reminiscent instead of the social dramas by the Norwegian playwright Henrik Ibsen, most famous for his experiments in realism and such works as *Peer Gynt, A Doll's House* and *Ghosts*. This new play is a densely layered response to the era's avant-gardism, with traces of symbolism, expressionism and futurism. In 1917, Bontempelli, along with Enrico Borioli and Mario Sironi, edited the futurist journal for the trenches, *Il Montello,* and then would write for *Roma futurista* and *L'Italia futurista*, which he had declared "the only political paper worth reading today"; all the others were too "bland, ironic, rational" when it came to the bourgeois cowards.[7] Combat over, Bontempelli went to live in Milan, where he spent his evenings at Margherita Sarfatti's exclusive salon. There he met the hostess's lover Benito Mussolini and become a contributor to *Ardita*, the cultural supplement to his newspaper *Il Popolo d'Italia*. Bontempelli was one of the founding members of the Futurist Political Party, which would receive an invitation from *Il Duce* to participate in the formation of the fascist movement in 1919. (Marinetti[8] and many of the futurist politicians would defect from Mussolini's *fasci* (fascist political groups)[9] when they took a turn to the right in 1920).

In 1919, at more than forty years of age, Bontempelli was a successful, prolific writer and, eschewing aestheticism in the name of revolution, he disinherited nearly everything he had published up until that time: all four plays and numerous volumes of poetry and fiction, with the exception of *Sette Savi* (*Seven Sages*, 1912). This was the first in a series of repudiations that would punctuate his career. It was a gesture typical of the futurists — who had

---

7. From a widely cited letter to Emilio Settimelli, first published in *L'Italia futurista*, December 9, 1917, 35.
8. Filippo Tommaso Marinetti (1876–1944), poet, playwright and founder, in 1909, of futurism.
9. The word *fascio* literally means a bundle; Mussolini's fascists *(fascisti)* borrowed the term and iconography of the ancient Roman bundle of rods with protruding axe. The word *fascio* (or plural *fasci*) was, however, commonly used to refer to political groups or leagues, and fasces still today frequently appear in governmental crests.

Introduction

famously abjured Gabriele D'Annunzio and the "symbolist masters, last lovers of the moon" — and of avant-gardism itself. But for Bontempelli, the gesture of refutation would eternally return. It would, indeed, define him as a writer and public intellectual. On the chopping block in 1919 weren't just single works, but the neck of old-school Bontempelli. Though he would later describe this moment as a "restless crisis of maturation," he wasn't in fact shunning immature works.[10] Instead, he was exorcising that part of himself that lived outside the fray. Later, Bontempelli would re-recognize the poetry of *Il Purosangue* (*The Thoroughbred*, 1919) and *Watching the Moon*. His rejection of the Carduccian poems and Dannunzian and naturalist dramas was the declaration that, like his futurist comrades, he too wanted to free Italy "from its smelly gangrene of professors, archaeologists, *ciceroni* and antiquarians,"[11] combat the symbolists' "romantic sentimentalism drenched with moonshine"[12] and turn art into "action-art."[13]

The train engineer's son had found a home with that futurist movement whose faith lay in the religion of speed. Two of Bontempelli's best loved works, *La vita intensa* and *La vita operosa* (*The Intense Life* and *The Industrious Life*), where Milan's hustle and bustle take center stage, date to the 1919–20 period, as does the highly original play for humans actors, puppets and marionettes, *Siepe a nordovest* (*Northwest Hedge*), which would be illustrated by Giorgio De Chirico, the famed metaphysical painter and scenographer, and produced at the inauguration of Anton Giulio Bragaglia's avant-garde Teatro degli Indipendenti in 1923. In 1920, some important personal ties were severed, too. Bontempelli separated from his wife, Amelia (Meletta) Della Pergola, whom he had married in 1909, because of her relationship with his

---

10. Note to *La guardia alla luna*, in Bontempelli, *Teatro* (Milano: Mondadori, 1947), 1:47.
11. "The Founding and Manifesto of Futurism," in *Futurist Manifestoes*, ed. Umbro Appollonio (Boston: Museum of Fine Arts, 2001), 22.
12. "Noi rinneghiamo i nostri maestri simbolisti ultimi amanti della luna" [We repudiate our symbolist masters, last lovers of the moonlight], in F.T. Marinetti, *Teoria e invenzione futurista* (Milan: Mondadori, 1968), 261.
13. "Futurist Reconstruction of the Universe 1915," in *Futurist Manifestoes*, 198.

Introduction

friend and fellow writer, De Chirico's brother, Alberto Savinio.[14] Bontempelli would remain on good terms with her, and they also remained married, since there was no divorce in Italy. After a period of bitterness, he reestablished the friendship with Savinio as well. References to both — and to a "marital disappointment" — would appear in *The Intense Life*, whose narrator-protagonist was Massimo, Bontempelli himself. (This was hardly a realist Massimo, it should be noted; for he was accompanied around town by both his friend Pietro and a Socratic daimôn who planted mischievous notions in his mind.)

But then futurism took its turn on the chopping block. When Bontempelli launched his own literary movement, Novecento (Twentieth Century), and its journal, *900: Cahiers d'Italie e d'Europe,* in September of 1926, his farewell to futurism would have been clear to any knowing reader, for the first issue's opening essay began with the assertion that the "most urgent and precise task of the twentieth century will be the reconstruction of time and space" — time and space, futurism had famously touted, "died yesterday."[15] Like his former *Montello* colleague Mario Sironi, head of the Novecento painters' movement established in 1922, Bontempelli hoped to usher in a twentieth-century renaissance, needed after the destruction of the Great War and the nihilism of the avant-garde. For this reason, his movement has been linked to the general European trend of the *rappel à l'ordre,* or "return to order," championed by such figures as Savinio in Italy, through the art magazine *Valori plastici,* and by Jean Cocteau in France. Walking away from cubism and futurism, the return to order marked a revival of realism in painting and also of classicism, if often of a metaphysical nature.[16] In Bontempelli's case, the classicism of his early years remained, not so much in poetic form — with the

---

14. Alberto Savinio (Andrea De Chirico, 1891–1952) was a writer, painter and musician who, like his brother and Bontempelli, experimented with various types of fantastic literature and art: surrealism, modern neoclassicism, metaphysical painting, etc. A founder of the movement and journal *Valori plastici,* he was a leading proponent of the artistic "return to order" in Italy.
15. "Giustificazione," in *AN*, 17. The *900* prefaces are also available in Bontempelli, *Opere scelte,* ed. Luigi Baldacci (Milan: Mondadori, 1997).
16. On Bontempelli and Novecento in France and the context of a return to classicism, see Edoardo Costadura, *D'un classicisme à l'autre: France–Italie, 1919–1939* (Saint-Denis: Presses Universitaires de Vincennes, 1999).

Introduction

exception of assorted verses within narrative and dramatic works, he ceased to write poetry — but in the pronounced desire to create "new myths for the modern age" and in the consequent use of stories or characters with the names and traits of those in ancient myth (to note just a few, Vulcan/Haephaestus, Narcissus, and, not surprisingly, the ever-regenerating Phoenix).

His attitude toward futurism was categorical:

> We profess a great admiration for futurism, which clearly and without regard has cut the bridges between the nineteenth and twentieth centuries. Without its principles and its audacity, the spirit of the old century, which prolonged its agony until the explosion of the war, even today would obstruct us: none of us Novecentists, if we hadn't passed through futurism's persuasion and passion, could today utter the words that open the new century.

Marinetti's movement had been a work of art, "the last and most dazzling expression of romanticism," he wrote, but the romantic epoch had now come to a close.[17]

This was a clear relegation of futurism not just to *his* past, but to *the* past (highlighted by his consistent use of that tense whenever he spoke of the movement). Bontempelli argued that there were three epochs of human history, and casting futurism as the last vestige of romanticism meant placing it squarely in the second, now defunct romantic age, which had extended from the birth of Christ until the Great War. The fathers had conquered and held the trenches — he was clear about this and expressed his admiration — but behind them he, the son, would "begin to build the city of the conquerors": that is to say, the literature of the third epoch.[18]

As a matter of fact, Bontempelli's star was on the rise. He would effectively emerge as one who "set the intellectual tone for the entire era."[19] He had moved to the capital in 1921 "because a respectable person who's reached the age of thirty goes to live in

---

17. From the preface to the June 1927 issue of *900*, "Analogies," in *AN*, 38.
18. Ibid., 41.
19. Jeffrey T. Schnapp, *Staging Fascism: 18 BL and the Theater of Masses for Masses* (Stanford, CA: Stanford University Press, 1996), 42.

Introduction

Rome," and throughout the decade as a public intellectual soared to unforeseen heights.[20] He was ever-present in the newspapers, writing in *Il Tempo, Il Mondo, Il Corriere della Sera* and *La Gazzetta del Popolo*. In 1925 one journalist referred to him as Italy's most talked-about writer.[21] Novecento reinforced his ties with the best and brightest, and most experimental, of European letters: *900* was first published in French — which gave it broad international exposure — and its editorial staff included such elites as Ramòn Gomez de la Serna, Georg Kaiser, Pierre Mac Orlan, Ilya Ehrenburg,[22] and most notably, James Joyce. The list of contributing talents is equally impressive: Joyce, Marinetti, Anton Chekhov, Rainer Maria Rilke, Leo Tolstoy, Virginia Woolf (this was her introduction to Italian readers) and a young Alberto Moravia, who would become one of Italy's most important novelists in the decades to follow. Under the Novecento rubric, Bontempelli adopted from art criticism the terms *realismo magico* — magic realism — to describe the literature he was after, a development of his earlier experiments in surrealism, seen in works like *La scacchiera davanti allo specchio* (*The Chess Set in the Mirror*, 1922) and *Eva Ultima* (*Last Eve*, 1923), that had clear ties to the metaphysics of painters like De Chirico and Carrà. Some of Bontempelli's best narratives date to the twenties, including the short story collections *La donna dei miei sogni* (*The Woman of My Dreams*, 1925) and *Il figlio di due madri* (*The Boy with Two Mothers*, 1929). It was also a golden decade for his playwriting. In April of 1925, the performance of *Nostra Dea* (*Our Goddess*), directed by none other than Luigi Pirandello for his Teatro d'Arte, of which Bontempelli was a founding member, caused critic Corrado Alvaro to proclaim that the Sicilian dramatist-cum-director "finally gave

---

20. As Bontempelli wrote to his friend, fellow writer Emilio Bodrero, November 23, 1921. In Simona Cigliana, "Due epistolari e un carteggio inediti," *L'Illuminista* 5.13–15 (2005): 34.
21. *Corriere Emiliano* (Parma), 1925. GRI 63.
22. Ramón Gómez de la Serna (1888–1963), Spanish experimental writer; George Kaiser (1878–1945), one of Germany's most important expressionist dramatists, emigrated to Switzerland in opposition to Nazism; Pierre Mac Orlan (Pierre Dumarchey, 1882–1970), French bohemian writer and songwriter, with various pseudonyms also wrote pornographic novels; Ilya Ehrenburg (1891–1967), important Soviet writer and journalist, traveled frequently to Europe and was the friend of such artists as Pablo Picasso and Diego Rivera.

us what we've been waiting for."[23] *Minnie la candida* (*Genuine Minnie*, 1928) caused quite the ruckus, sparking a war between the halves of a divided public, and the reprised *Watching the Moon* finally triumphed. Bontempelli would later sigh that it typically took critics ten years to understand him; in this case he was right. Fascinated by the cinema, too, our twentieth-century renaissance man founded Rome's first cineclub in 1929.

But when he presented himself as the post-futurist who would lead the way, the grown son of a train engineer wasn't just carving out his own space in the world of Italian letters. He was — consciously and explicitly — promoting himself and his Novecento colleagues as the new voices of the epoch under construction: the fascist one. His admiration for Mussolini, to whom he would send a book with the dedication, "To the super-fast duce,"[24] extended back to the Milanese salon years, and his antidemocratic nationalism even further. Like so many of his generation who were impatient with and downright disgusted by the corrupt and tepid parliamentary bargaining of liberal, bourgeois Italian politics, he saw in fascism the potential for a revolution that was at the same time cultural, social and political. In the first few years of Mussolini's rule, Bontempelli had reiterated an avant-gardist faith in the power of art, stating that il Duce's best instruments were the new artists and writers.[25] And around the time of the Teatro d'Arte premiere, in a *Popolo d'Italia* interview with Luigi Freddi, Bontempelli declared himself "at least in spirit, fascist," because he was "at least in spirit, revolutionary. Italy needed a big war and a big revolution. It had the war. It still needs the revolution. I'm with you, with all my heart, as long as you allow me to hope that you'll make it."[26]

However, Bontempelli's was a fiercely independent soul. He opted not to sign the Manifesto of fascist intellectuals penned by philosopher Giovanni Gentile in 1925. Years later, Mussolini would express disappointment over this choice but note that fascism aimed

---

23. Corrado Alvaro, "'Nostra Dea' di Bontempelli," in *Cronache e scritti teatrali*, ed. Alfredo Barbina (Rome: Abete, 1976), 91.
24. Conserved in the Archivio centrale dello stato, Roma, Segreteria particolare del duce carteggio ordinario 209.
25. Bontempelli, *Il neosofista e altri scritti* (Milan: Mondadori, 1929), 13.
26. Massimo Bontempelli, interview with Luigi Freddi, *Il Popolo d'Italia*, April 1925, GRI 63.

Introduction

for "consensus," not "vendetta," and thus all was copacetic.[27] Nor would Bontempelli initially join the National Fascist Party (PNF), but this didn't prevent him from being named Secretary of the Fascist Writers' Union in 1926 or from having Mussolini's help in a nomination to the Royal Academy of Italian Academics in 1930. He received his party membership card in 1935, when all Academics not possessing it were presented with one.[28]

Formalities aside, truth be told, his "spiritual" adhesion to the movement in the early-mid 1920s was unequivocal. When the journal *Critica fascista* hosted a debate on fascist culture in 1926–27 — how to create one and what it should look like — Bontempelli threw his hat into the ring, offering Novecento as the regime's best bet. Nothing of the "rotting leftovers of psychological analysis, of naturalism, of aestheticism, of petty bourgeois tastes, of nauseating and fraudulent sentimentalism" would be appropriate for fascism:

> The new art must be entertaining, even when its roots are suffering; it must cover with smiles the saddest of things and with wonder the most banal. It must be a miracle rather than a chore, an act of magic rather than the bustle of official business. It must rediscover a sense of mystery and the equilibrium between earth and sky.[29]

---

27. Yvon De Begnac, *Taccuini mussoliniani*, ed. Francesco Perfetti (Bologna: Il Mulino, 1990), 286.

28. Most scholars have reported that Bontempelli joined the PNF when Pirandello did in 1924, but there is no record of this, and several testimonies to the contrary exist (including newspapers of the period that note his non-membership). The writer himself contributed to this confusion, at times referring to his "adhesion" to the movement, which many have been taken as official membership. The postwar testimonies of Bontempelli's long-time companion, Paola Masino, regarding his fascism must be taken with caution, as she consistently downplays his attachment to the party and its hierarchs, but in this case she provides the missing detail that it was through the Academy that Bontempelli finally officially joined the party in 1935. See Giuseppe Grieco, "La vita di Massimo Bontempelli," *Gente* (November 1975): 67. Museo d'Arte Moderna & Contemporanea di Trento e Rovereto (MART) Fondo Belli. On Gentile's manifesto of fascist intellectuals and Croce's counter-manifesto, see Francesco Dei, "Il firmamento: Appelli e dichiarazioni collettive," in *Atlante della letteratura italiana* 3, ed. Sergio Luzzatto and Gabriele Pedullà (Turin: Einaudi, 2012), 734–43.

29. An abridged English version of Bontempelli's essay, along with several others from the cultural debates, is partially reprinted in Jeffrey

Introduction

What he had to say here would have sounded quite familiar to anyone who had read the September issue of *900*, but just in case anyone missed it, he closed his piece thus: "Without wanting to, caro Bottai [the journal's creator and director, then vice-secretary of the fascist corporations], I've more or less repeated 900's program to you. It was inevitable."[30]

And yet, Bontempelli had little luck imposing Novecento as the fascist art par excellence, for others disagreed, seeing in its principles the antithesis of all fascism stood for. Its founder — who didn't want to produce or disseminate propaganda but did wish to promote the movement as an ideal expression of fascism — found himself navigating troubled waters. The hungriest sharks were ex-co-founder Curzio Malaparte, Mino Maccari and the ultra-conservative *Strapaese* (Super Village) group, who promoted native cultural models in opposition to foreign impulses. *Strapaese* accused Bontempelli of "diffusing a modernist culture designed for and by 'Jews and Pederasts,'" begrudging him the variety of collaborators — homegrown and foreign, blackshirt and non-fascist alike — and especially the choice to publish in French.[31] Their attacks were obviously geared to suggest that Novecento lacked the patriotism that a fascist artistic movement would require.

The troubles for *900* began even before the first issue was released. When Bontempelli circulated "Justifications," its theoretical preface, it provoked complaints from both sides. For the nationalist, extremist fascist contingent, it wasn't fascist enough; for the journal's Parisian secretary Nino Frank, it was too fascist and therefore a big risk. *900* had the potential to become the most important literary magazine of the day, but if it turned out to be a party organ, the broader European literary public was apt to lose interest, and powerhouse teammates like Joyce, Mac Orlan, and others would surely defect. Mussolini was going to weigh in, but, Bontempelli knew, if il Duce lent his support, which he did, the uber-fascist opponents would be hushed, but then, "that cock

---

T. Schnapp, *A Primer of Italian Fascism* (Lincoln: University of Nebraska, 2000), 218–20. When possible citations of it to this point are taken from that volume.

30. *Critica fascista* 4.22 (November 15, 1926): 417.

31. For a brief discussion of this duel, plus a consideration of magic realism within the myriad of realisms that emerged in the thirties, see Ruth Ben-Ghiat, *Fascist Modernities: Italy 1922–1945* (Berkeley: University of California Press, 2001), 25–29 and chapter two.

Introduction

and bull story about the 'journal of fascist propaganda in French' [could] seem true!"[32]

In reality, Mussolini's backing didn't silence anyone. Bontempelli's critics were relentless. And then, il Duce grew tired of his name being bandied about. The regime encouraged debate but preferred a policy of aesthetic pluralism, and he didn't appreciate it when artists spoke for him. In July of 1929, he had some harsh words for Sarfatti's encouragement of those who tried "to suggest that Fascism's artistic position is that of your *'900"*:

> Since you don't yet possess the elementary reserve to avoid mixing up my name as a politician with your would-be artistic inventions, don't be surprised if, at the first opportunity given me and in the most explicit way, I specify my position and that of Fascism in regards to the so-called '900 or what remains of the late '900.[33]

Bontempelli was careful to distinguish his own movement from Sarfatti and Sironi's, but it's perhaps no coincidence that in this period *900* finally ceased publication, and that Bontempelli's appeals to il Duce to help him keep his post as secretary of the writer's union — threatened by the ongoing feuds — evidently fell on deaf ears.[34]

But neither *900*'s closure nor Bontempelli's relocation to Paris for most of 1930–31 dimmed the luminary's glow.[35] As mentioned

---

32. Letter from Bontempelli to Nino Frank, Rome, December 5, 1926, in Corrado Alvaro, Massimo Bontempelli, and Nino Frank, *Lettere a "900,"* ed. Marinella Mascia Galateria (Rome: Bulzoni, 1985), 111.
33. Cited in Simona Cigliana, "Una lunga 'avventura': Bontempelli a Bodrero, a Meletta (ovvero da *Eva Futura* a *Eva Ultima*), a Mussolini, 'Duce velocissimo,'" *L'Illuminista* 5.13–15 (2005): 166.
34. Bontempelli and his two closest collaborators (now Gian Gaspare Napolitano and Giulio Santangelo) decided to close the review after the June 1929 issue was released; it had suffered from the polemics, especially when these pushed Bontempelli to publish in Italian only, which greatly diminished the enthusiasm of his international contributors. Napolitano also speculated that it was hard for people to wrap their heads around the idea of a non-fascist fascist magazine: that is to say, one that "interpreted the word of Mussolini" but received no backing from his government. See Corrado Donati, "Massimo Bontempelli e '900': un numero inedito tra due profezie," in *Massimo Bontempelli scrittore e intellettuale,* ed. Corrado Donati (Rome: Editori Riuniti, 1992), 187–204, at 198.
35. He left with his new love interest, Paola Masino, whose family was greatly distressed by the relationship (not only was Bontempelli married, he was thirty years Masino's senior).

Introduction

above, he was appointed to the Academy of Intellectuals in 1930, with Mussolini's support. On this occasion, once again it was remarked that "he doesn't carry the party card but spiritually is fascist."[36] In the new decade, Bontempelli created the architecture magazine *Quadrante* (1933) with P.M. Bardi and continued to write inexhaustibly, publishing, among others, a novel about a day in the life of a 522 model Fiat and her — the car is decidedly feminine — owner Bruno, *522: Storia di una giornata* (*522: Story of a Day*, 1932); the travel chronicle *Pezzi di mondo* (*Pieces of the World*, 1935); one of his most enduring novels, *Gente nel tempo* (*People through Time*, 1937) and four more plays, though none of these would have the success *Nostra Dea* did. The demise of *900* didn't slow his stride abroad either. Samuel Putnam, a journalist, translator and co-editor with Ezra Pound of the *New Review* — to which Bontempelli contributed — wrote about Bontempelli "practically every week" in his column for the *New York Sun*.[37] The American literary magazine *The Living Age* published five of the author's pieces between 1926 and 1930. And Bontempelli's renunciation of *La Piccola* didn't keep it from being staged in London in 1930. Nor was it uncommon to see Bontempelli written about in T.S. Eliot's *Criterion*.[38] Meanwhile, Bontempelli traveled extensively, giving lectures on Italian literature and culture in the Mediterranean, in Eastern Europe and, most significantly for the history of fantastic literature, in South America.

But another rupture was in the works. It would announce itself in 1938, although it didn't lack foreshadowing. Two of Bontempelli's acts have garnered much attention by scholars, as evidence of a definitive break with Mussolini's regime. First, he declined a professorship in Italian literature at the University of Florence, offered to him when newly implemented racial laws ousted the prestigious Jewish literary critic and scholar, Attilio Momigliano, from the post. Then, in late November, Bontempelli gave a speech at Pescara commemorating the deceased Gabriele D'Annunzio, which landed him in hot water, especially with PNF secretary Achille

---

36. "Significato di Bontempelli," *Corriere di Sicilia* (Catania), October 24, 1930, n.p. GRI 66, 7.
37. Cigliana, "Due epistolari," 86.
38. *The Criterion*, published from 1922 to 1939 was a leading literary journal of the period. It published many of the epoch's best authors, including Virginia Woolf, Ezra Pound, Luigi Pirandello, Marcel Proust and Paul Valéry.

Starace. A few months later, he was prohibited from conducting any professional activity — putting him in dire financial straits — his party card and passport were revoked, distribution of the volume containing the problematic speech and another book, *L'avventura novecentista (Twentieth-Century Adventure)*, was prohibited, and he was forced to leave Rome, taking up residence in Venice.

For decades, a mythic version of these events prevailed, in which the writer was sent to *confino* (fascism's system of house arrest for subversives) in Venice for his bald acts of rebellion. However, the punishment was never so severe, nor was Bontempelli's behavior unambiguous. First, his refusal to accept Momigliano's professorship is easily interpreted as a stand against the anti-Jewish legislation, and it is true that these measures were highly unpopular among the intelligentsia. Yet it is hardly so clear that Bontempelli's choice either produced friction with the fascist hierarchy or was evidence of his discontent; a letter from Masino to her mother reveals that when Bottai offered Bontempelli the post, he said he would think about it, and perhaps eventually accept, the next year.[39]

When it comes to the Pescara speech, scholars have identified its references to the contemporary world's "military obedience," "cultivated barbarism" and "fetishization of violence" as the incriminating passages: those that revealed Bontempelli's change in heart toward fascism and brought this severe disciplinary action against him. What's noteworthy, however, is that his troubles didn't begin immediately; two months after the event, Bottai recorded in his diary doubt that the speech — or speeches, for there was some talk about one on Leopardi, given well over a year before — was "intellectual antifascism" and remarked that the reasons for punishment were "vague."[40] From a letter Bontempelli wrote in his own defense, we learn that Starace's complaints were quibbles — one passage contained no reference to Mussolini, another suggested that D'Annunzio was greater than il Duce, another still drew an unfavorable parallel — that had nothing to do with the "cultivated barbarism" or "fetishization of violence" that today sound like clear jabs at fascism.

---

39. Paola Masino, *Io, Massimo e gli altri: Autobiografia di una figlia del secolo* (Milan: Rusconi, 1995), 79.
40. Giuseppe Bottai, *Diario 1935–1944*, ed. Giordano Bruno Guerri (Milan: Rizzoli, 2001), 140.

Introduction

Bontempelli was dismayed that his speech could have been interpreted as critical of the regime, and truth be told, a careful reading of the exceedingly dense piece, which doesn't entirely lack ambiguity, speaks in his favor. The anti-democratic and anti-bourgeois Bontempelli, who had approved of the blackshirt cudgel and greeted the regime's imperialism with enthusiasm, can't be assumed to have been criticizing the epoch when he characterized it as a time of transition from "vain individualism to a hankering for military obedience, from a presumed inalterable peace to war ever-ready."[41] A *characterization* of fascism as violent, in short, isn't from every point of view a *criticism* of fascism as violent, and there aren't many reasons to think that it was so in Bontempelli's case. The language of "barbarism," moreover, was one popular in the revolutionary circles that gave rise to fascism. In that context, it was a generational battle: youth's uprising against the old was hailed as a return of barbarism — of instinctive energies, pure ideas, rigid morality. It's noteworthy, in fact, that Bontempelli, who perpetually considered himself on the side of the young, used language so similar to that of fellow writer and Mussolini fan Giuseppe Prezzolini, who described il Duce's spirit as a "sort of controlled barbarism."[42]

This is perhaps why it wasn't difficult for Bontempelli to redeem himself. By the fall of 1939, he was back in the regime's good graces, his party card was restored to him, he could publish again, and his new releases were back on store shelves. He continued to live in Venice, and though he had been told to leave Rome, he had never actually been under arrest, as personal and government documents prove. Moreover, Bontempelli began to work with fascist officials again. He was invited to give a talk on Verga, an event as important as the Pirandello or D'Annunzio speeches had been. And more significantly still, he received 20,000 lire from the minister of popular culture, Dino Alfieri, as clear compensation for the financially trying months and advanced payment "for the

---

41. Bontempelli, "D'Annunzio o del martirio," in *Opere scelte*, 861–93.
42. On barbarism in revolutionary syndicalism, see Emilio Gentile, *Le origini dell'ideologia fascista 1918–1925* (Bologna: Il Mulino, 1996), 135–38. Available in English as *The Origins of Fascist Ideology, 1918–1925* (New York: Enigma, 2005). For Prezzolini, see Daniela Brogi, *Giovani: Vita e scrittura tra fascismo e dopoguerra* (Palermo: Duepunti, 2012), 56.

Introduction

collaboration you'll still want to offer me" — a declaration of the regime's desire to normalize relations.[43] All of this suggests that Bontempelli's actions in this period, rather than concerted efforts to "break up," are better viewed, at most, as attempts to speak his peace on fundamental issues: as he always had done, in plain terms and with relative impunity. Now, with Pirandello and D'Annunzio both dead, in fact, Bontempelli had more clout than ever; but perhaps he overestimated just how much.

At the same time, even if the D'Annunzio speech wasn't quite the watershed it's been presented to be, Bontempelli was undoubtedly at a crossroads in late 1938; the direction he would take eventually led him to the Communist Party, with whom he would establish ties certainly by the time the Mussolini government fell in 1943 (but when, exactly, isn't yet clear). Interestingly enough, the one declaration by the writer that hasn't received attention from scholars is in some ways the clearest expression of mounting disillusionment. As clearly as Bontempelli had offered Novecento in 1926 as the ideal art form of the fascist revolution, he would present his new release, *L'avventura novecentista*, which came out within days of the Pescara speech, as his departure from all of that. In his November foreword to the volume, which collected his *900* writings and others from '29 to '33, he wrote that the book documented "a state of mind inclined to seek harmony between the literary and the political, and represents a personal experience by now decidedly concluded: I could call it my 'Roman experience.'"[44] A few months later, he would indeed move from the capital city, but the preface also indicated another sort of leave-taking from the regime headquartered there: Bontempelli's walking away from over two decades of trying to find the ideal fusion of politics and art. For one who had proffered his movement as the fascist art par excellence, this was a radical departure indeed — whatever his reasons for it were.

Still, Bontempelli's next poetic repudiation matched his political one, betraying a continued desire to square the circle (and

---

43. Letter from Dino Alfieri to Bontempelli, 8 October 1939, GRI 7. Cigliana has addressed the *confino* issue and the ambiguities of this period, though she still characterizes the rupture as definitive: see "Una lunga avventura," 175–83.
44. The citation comes from *AN,* preface (n.p). It is omitted from Jacobbi's 1974 edition.

Introduction

perhaps suggesting that he had indeed grown restless with fascism, not merely with attempts to ideally fuse politics and aesthetics). The cry couldn't have been more explicit. It came from the mouth of the fairy godmother in the 1942 *Cenerentola* (*Cinderella*, the final play in this collection, which premiered at the Florentine Maggio Musicale festival that year). "Enough. Enough. Enough with magic!" she cries, and although using her powers one last time to send Cinderella to the royal ball, she rejoices when her goddaughter renounces all that the magic slipper might have given her: the young maiden rejects the prince in favor of Icarus, the court's poor viola player.

Reading the play as a political allegory, no one would have been surprised that its author, in the years since the turbulence with fascist hierarchy, had sought and established contact with the Italian Communists. More astute readers — or spectators — would have seen even more. When Bontempelli had his fairy godmother lay down her wand, he put into her words and deeds a renunciation of the magic that he had championed as a means of creating fascist art. This time the renunciation is different, for it is not Massimo Bontempelli narrator or critic — who at times, but not always, overlap — who speaks it, but one of his characters; and, in fact, magic wouldn't entirely disappear from his works. The fairy godmother's deed we might read then as an enactment of her creator's defining behavior rather than another instance of it. At the same time, her declarations — "Fairy? To be a fairy, you just have to know you are one," and "The greatest magic is intelligence" — would find echoes the next year (June 1943) in Bontempelli-critic's *Tempo* column, where he lamented that people wouldn't forget about the terms "Novecentismo" and "realismo magico," when he himself had already "finished a while ago: finished, I mean, using this formula, 'magic realism,'" which he had in any case employed "in a provisory and polemical manner," never with an intent to "construct or delineate systems." There were no more magicians, only artists. It was all about imagination, for "magic in a strict sense is nothing more than art in a rough state."[45]

It's true, this wasn't a wholesale negation of magic. But it's just as true that with such proclamations Bontempelli formally shunned the magic realism recipe that he had for so long explicitly tied to the

---

45. Bontempelli, "Che cos'è il realismo magico?" *Tempo* (Milan), June 24, 1943, 4. GRI 69.

Introduction

would-be fascist revolution. One of the reasons that Bontempelli's theatrical opus seems so significant in his literary journey is that we see much more clearly there — especially in a play like his 1947 *Venezia Salva*, a re-elaboration of Thomas Otway's *Venice Preserved* (1682) — a real effort to reinvent himself and his art, once again. If he had dramatized such an effort in *Cinderella*, he would only achieve it for himself later, with the Venetian tragedy.

When the fascist government fell in July of 1943, Bontempelli and Masino returned to Rome. Several months later, when the Nazis had sprung il Duce from prison and implemented the Republic of Salò in the north, dividing Italy in a civil war, the fascists placed a bounty on Bontempelli's head — an indication of how full his political conversion was — and issued an exile order for Masino, who had written several works the censors had taken unkindly to. The two went into hiding until Rome's liberation in 1944 and after the war relocated to Milan, and later Venice, strengthening ties with the Communist Party.

In 1948, Bontempelli was elected senator for the Popular Front, founded that same year by the unification of the Communist and Socialist parties. But his fascist past would shadow him. Given a post-war law that prohibited any ex-blackshirt propagandist from taking public office, his election was challenged because he had edited a school textbook that contained passages now considered unacceptable. And, in truth, he had of his own accord designed a politically-slanted anthology of writings and had even pleaded for permission to include some of il Duce's own essays.[46] Despite the unwavering support of reputable anti-fascist intellectuals and politicians like Moravia, the publisher Giulio Einaudi (son of president of the Republic Luigi Einaudi) and Communist Party leader Palmiro Togliatti, he lost his seat. The purging of ex-fascists from the government was a matter of serious contention in post-war Italy and had been conducted in a rather haphazard and inconsistent matter. Bontempelli's case raised hackles partly because the laws seemed so much more intransigently applied in his case than in so many others. While a number of ex-fascist government officials managed to remain in office despite obvious violation of the statutes, the writer — who had never held an official government post and hadn't even enrolled in the PNF until

---

46. Cigliana, "Due epistolari," 92–96.

essentially forced to — was struck down. But this is only further testament to his prominence as a fascist intellectual and to the perception of him at least until the mid-to-late thirties as one of "those men closer to us than many who flaunt their fascist badges but maintain a democratic and liberal attitude that reveals itself in every word and gesture."[47]

In other words, notwithstanding muffled nonconformist yelps like refusing to join the party or neglecting to sign the manifesto, Bontempelli's status as one of the regime's chief men of culture was undisputed. Inevitably, then, his conversion was too much for some to believe or bear, as a fragment from one 1950 letter to the "ex-senator" testifies:

> You are good as a poet, but even better as the king of chameleons.
> As regards your famous commandments, that is to say,
> 1) I believe in the fascist revolution
> 2) I believe in the blackshirts
> 3) I believe in Mussolini, God without prophets, etc. etc.
>
> what do you have to say? You'll tell me that you said these things ten years ago, but the name that pronounced them and the pen that wrote them are always the same. And so, were you a liar then, or are you a liar now?[48]

Certainly a stinging accusation for a man who had been, always, outspoken, in his views. Although from a contemporary (especially American) perspective, the "king of chameleons" charge seems temptingly appropriate not only for a writer who had gone from classicism to futurism to magic realism, but also and especially from fascism to communism, we might look at Massimo Bontempelli differently. For the vast majority of his career, his behavior wasn't that of a chameleon who changes his color for protection's sake, but of a serpent who outgrows and then sheds an uncomfortable skin. Like that serpent, who rubs his head against a rock to rupture that casing and wriggle out of it, Bontempelli, too, fought each time to grow out of one skin and into another. As he had explained his 1919 renunciation of his earlier works, he "felt compelled to destroy all of [his] past in order to be free to start

---

47. "Significato di Bontempelli," n.p.
48. Letter from Anna Arrigoni to Bontempelli, Milan, June 30, 1950, GRI 60, 1. Letters of support from the above-mentioned figures are found here as well.

Introduction

again."[49] Looking to the Popular Front was about starting again. It was about keeping hope for a revolution alive — Bontempelli was hardly alone in this among intellectuals during that very tragic period in Italian life. His slamming the door on Mussolini and setting off down the walk to Togliatti was less a migration from one end of the political spectrum to the other than it was his political life coming full circle. After fascism fell, the battle was between the leftist front and the liberal Christian Democratic party, which won the elections that year and would dominate Italian politics for decades to come. The left coalition was the natural, logical choice for a Bontempelli who had always been and continued to be anti-liberal, antibourgeois and revolutionary. Many years later, Silvio D'Amico's[50] son Fedele would remember that his father's friend, Bontempelli, had been fascist for the same reason he had first been futurist: both movements had rebelled against "the degenerate bourgeois spirit, for example, in late romanticism or positivism, or in the contradictions of the democracies in power."[51] The writer's conversion to communism was a repudiation of his fascist past, which anyone who had lived through those two decades had legitimate reason to question, but it was also a refusal to go back to the political models of old. The train engineer's son would never have travelled backward in time. And though the aforementioned *Venezia Salva* betrayed metaphysics in line with the existentialism of Jean Paul Sartre — whom Bontempelli palled around with in Venice in the late 40s — it also vindicated his preference, unwavering, for revolution, which in his eyes fascism had promised but failed to deliver. In the forties, it was in the other regime that Bontempelli placed his hope. Like the Novecentists who couldn't have built the city of the conquerors without futurism first

---

49. Note to *La guardia alla luna*, in Bontempelli, *Teatro*, 1:47.
50. Silvio D'Amico was one of Italy's most authoritative theater critics and, having had close ties to a number of fascist hierarchs, quite powerful in the theater industry at the time.
51. Fedele D'Amico, "Aveva un sol torto: non era un provinciale," *L'Espresso* (January 1979) cited in *Lettere a Ruggero Jacobbi: Registro di un fondo inedito con un appendice di lettere,* ed Francesca Bartolini (Florence: Firenze University Press, 2006). This article was written in defense of Bontempelli, who was attacked for his fascism when the Mondadori *Opere scelte* edited by Luigi Baldacci was released. The attack by Mario Picchi sparked a polemic, which saw nine literati – including Baldacci, Eugenio Montale and Enzo Siciliano — objecting to the gratuitous tone of Picchi's comments.

cutting the bridges, he himself couldn't move forward until he had bid decisive adieu.

Bontempelli would largely retire from public life and from publishing after the Senate debacle. In 1950 he had, after all, reached the ripe age of 72. Though *Gente nel tempo* had met with some success and received a stage adaptation in 1949 by Giorgio Strehler, postwar Italy's most important director, little new writing emerged, and neither *Venezia Salva* nor Bontempelli's last play, *L'innocenza di Camilla* (*Camilla's Innocence*, 1949) found great fortune. Despite the writer's obvious fall from grace, his short story collection *L'amante fedele* (*The Faithful Lover*) won the prestigious Strega Prize in 1953. With a handful of loyal friends and Masino by his side, Massimo Bontempelli passed the last years of his life in relative quiet and solitude, dying of what was probably Alzheimer's on July 21, 1960.

Reconstructing the Universe: Futurism, Novecento and the Avant-Garde

Silvio D'Amico once confessed, "I've only been afraid three times in my life: the first was in the war when I found myself stranded in an air raid [...]; the second was in New York on a roller coaster that seemed to have gone haywire; the third was when Massimo Bontempelli wanted to show off his daredevil driving."[52] There's no doubt about it: Bontempelli had a futurist love of speed, and yet his passion for vehicles and motors was shadowed sometimes by melancholic introspection and at other times by uneasy irony regarding the futurist universe that was the new reality.

In the three-act drama *Minnie la candida* — adapted from Bontempelli's own short story *Giovane anima credula* (*Naive Young Soul*, 1924) — the title character begins to believe that she is a robot, thanks to a joke played on her by her friend Tirreno, who tells her that some goldfish she sees are mechanical, electric — not real. Reasoning it through, she observes, "A little mechanical fish is completely perfect, but a real one has a head that's a bit too big [...] men and women, when they're real, all have

---

52. Grieco, "La vita di Massimo Bontempelli," 70.

Introduction

a thing that is a little funny, that doesn't fit quite right and makes you laugh."⁵³ Unable to find in herself something that doesn't fit quite right — and thus convinced that she is mechanical, too — Minnie commits suicide, plunging from a balcony to her death while an electric cityscape radiates behind her. The play's jab at futurism, which advocated for the ultimate "identification of man with motor,"⁵⁴ is sharp indeed. Like *Nostra Dea* before it, it is a meditation on the crisis of subjectivity in a post-futurist world: post-futurist not in the sense that futurism existed no longer, but in that the world had been forever changed by it. Recapturing subjectivity was a fundamental task of Novecento, directly tied to a post-futurist rebirth. Time and space had been destroyed, but once they were rebuilt, subjectivity would be, too: "the individual, sure of himself, sure of being himself, of being himself and not others," would be rediscovered.⁵⁵

As mentioned, Novecento has been classified under the *rappel à l'ordre* umbrella, and in keeping with that logic, Minnie's creator labeled a "moderate" avant-garde. As postwar Italy's most important Bontempelli scholar, Luigi Baldacci, described it, an avant-garde "that has from the start renounced its own aggressive purpose." ⁵⁶ There has been general consensus on this point, and Bontempelli's life is the story of one who passed through an avant-garde phase and then settled down. (The notion of a moderate avant-garde is an oxymoron; however, in essential agreement with Baldacci, most scholars have preferred to describe Bontempelli as a "modernist" but not an "avantgardist.") Also in part due to the irony toward Marinetti's movement even in Bontempelli's "most futurist" works, his output has been judged as lacking the exuberance — both formal and philosophical — of futurist exemplars. Put another way, seen in the context of the "return to order," his refutation of futurism has been essentially understood as a rejection of the avant-garde *per se*.

On avant-gardism, Bontempelli minced no words: that wasn't what he was up to. In his mind, the avant-garde didn't open the new epoch, it closed the old, and he and his movement were

---

53. *Minnie la candida,* in *Opere scelte,* 722.
54. "L'uomo moltiplicato e il regno della macchina," in Marinetti, *Teoria e invenzione,* 256.
55. "Giustificazione," 17.
56. Luigi Baldacci, *Massimo Bontempelli* (Turin: Borla, 1967), 65.

Introduction

harbingers of the new era.[57] Nonetheless, it can't escape our notice that in his own terms, Bontempelli was the consummate avant-gardist, for the moment of rupture, the gesture of repudiation, the wave goodbye and the slamming door absolutely defined his life and career. Likewise, had Bontempelli conceived of avant-gardism in the standard and etymological way — as that group on the front lines, advancing — he could have considered himself a standard bearer, post-futurism, for what was Novecento to do if not lead a new charge? It is with good reason that Renato Poggioli, one of the fathers of avant-garde theory, considered Bontempelli a major player, and one who possessed the psychological and social "agonism" that was crucial for the avant-garde, who "were conscious of being the precursors of the art of the future." This knowledge Poggioli called "futurism," and it was something all of the avant-gardists, not just the ones who took its name, shared.[58]

This is how Bontempelli's repudiation of futurism ought to be read: not, that is, as a rejection of the avant-garde *tout court*, but on the contrary as an avant-gardist's proclamation. Although his stance on futurism is meaningful for its content as well — by which I mean its depiction of futurism as lacking palingenetic potential — it is equally, if not more, important *as a gesture*. The discarding of futurism from the pages of *900* in 1926 was an agonistic cry that replicated the futurist's abjuration of D'Annunzio and the French symbolists. It mimicked Bontempelli's own renunciation of his earliest works. It prefigured his repudiation of the magic realist formula. It was, in the very same way, a gesture that signaled the break between old and new, and as Walter Adamson has characterized it in the case of futurism, a launching pad for a

---

57. See, for example, "Il vecchio spettacolo, come la pensavo nel '28," in *AN*, 353–56.
58. Renato Poggioli, *The Theory of the Avant-Garde*, trans. Gerald Fitzgerald (Cambridge, MA: Belknap Press of Harvard University Press, 1968; repr. New York: Harper & Row, 1971), 69, 61–74. A seductive metaphor for avant-gardism is provided by Walter Pedullà, in *Il morbo di Basedow ovvero dell'avanguardia* (Cosenza: Lerici 1975), where Graves' disease, which carries with it symptoms of hyperthyroidism, becomes that disease which the avant-garde hopes to contract and spread: a disease whose chief symptom is "the desire to run toward the precipice." This is a particularly apt image for Bontempelli's exhaustive aesthetic self-reinventing.

Introduction

new "cultural trajectory" that also served to surpass the anxiety of influence each of the avant-gardes inevitably feels.[59]

From this point of view, we should resist the temptation to view Bontempelli's work, and its avant-garde credentials, solely vis-à-vis the movement that preceded it. If the avant-garde is about moving forward, it ought not to be defined just in terms of what came before but in terms of its attitude about the present and the future. While it's true that Bontempelli dedicated enough space to Marinetti's movement in the *900* critical essays to make them seem like anti-futurist manifestoes,[60] he repeatedly praised futurism and its destructive, iconoclastic actions, which were necessary in their time: a time for him clearly superceded.

Though Bontempelli adopted the language of "construction" in describing his purposes, his disavowal of futurism wasn't about an aversion to its destructive methods or aggressive nature, and for this reason too, the image of the author as a moderate is unsatisfying. An analysis limited to the stylistic would inevitably characterize Bontempelli's fictional works as such in relation to select futurist pieces. His sophisticated prose was a far cry from futurist onomatopoeic word games. His full-length plays, though often episodic, seemed more traditional in their structure than the ultra-short futurist *sintesi* (syntheses). The delightful graphic tricks he used, while bursting forth from the pages of his novels, looked like faint echoes of the futurist manifestoes that were splayed across newspaper pages. But such analyses also only take into account the most extreme of futurist experiments. Held up to the most radical pieces, much futurist production would be considered as "moderate" as Bontempelli's. More importantly, Bontempelli-critic

---

59. Walter Adamson, "The End of an Avant-Garde? Filippo Tommaso Marinetti and Futurism in World War I and Its Aftermath," in *A History of Futurism: The Precursors, Protagonists, and Legacies*, ed. Geert Buelens, Harald Hendrix, and Michelangela Monica Jansen (Lanham, MD: Lexington Books, 2012), 302. The poets' "anxiety of influence" was first discussed by Harold Bloom in a book of the same title (New York: Oxford University Press, 1973). On the importance of the gesture — of public provocation — as a method of rupture in the art-historical tradition, see Boris Groys, *Introduction to Antiphilosophy*, trans. David Fernbach (London: Verso, 2012), 206–7.

60. Antonio Saccone, "'La trincea avanzata' e 'la città dei conquistatori': Bontempelli e l'avanguardia futurista," in Donati, ed., *Massimo Bontempelli scrittore e intellettuale*, 127–45.

Introduction

— the Bontempelli of the "manifesto" — was anything but mild or non-combative. He wrote that art needed to move toward "virile ugliness," literati were "pseudo-men," fascism had taught that sometimes "the only good thing to do is use the cudgel."[61]

The language of another Italian writer, Giuseppe Antonio Borgese, is one antidote to the tendency to "downgrade" Bontempelli's iconoclasm. In 1923, Borgese wrote of the "time to construct" (*tempo di edificare*), and both of these — time and reconstruction — were key concepts for Bontempelli. As scholars of fascist culture have highlighted, in 1920s Italy, tradition was not an impediment to innovation in the artistic sphere. Quite the opposite, attempts to recapture aspects of the great Italian tradition and model them in new ways, in modernist forms, were terrifically fruitful. Even when he recycled ancient myths, Bontempelli wasn't seeking moderation. He wasn't trying to "return," but to rise again, to build again, content to do so after futurism had left a blank slate. If today the concept of the *rappel à l'ordre*, helps us classify or contextualize Bontempelli's works — whose use of realism (magical and metaphysical) and classic elements (like myth) does admittedly reflect the trend of that moment — it perhaps does less than *tempo di edificare* to get to the heart of what he really wanted to do.[62]

Bontempelli's beef with futurism was quite straightforward. From his point of view, it just wasn't that useful or innovative anymore. And in this there's nothing so strange. Seventeen years separated the launching of futurism and Novecento. His assault on Marinetti's invention was analogous to the attack on the "age-old enemy," the bourgeoisie he had castigated in 1915 for going to the theater for distraction, when action was what was necessary.[63] He claimed that the futurists had become a group of artists concerned with formal innovation and the creation of masterpieces identifiable with them, while Novecento aspired to create "the myths and fables needed by the new times," whose stories and characters would be

---

61. "Fondamenti," "Consigli," and "Dovere dello scrittore," in *AN*, 25, 30, 293.
62. Giuseppe Antonio Borgese, *Tempo di edificare* (Milan: Fratelli Treves, 1923). Borgese was a much more traditional, nineteenth-century type of writer, so it is his formula rather than his actual work that applies for contextualizing Bontempelli.
63. Bontempelli, "Ho scritto 'Galleria degli schiavi,'" *La Gazzetta del Popolo*, November 14, 1934, now in Bontempelli, *Racconti e romanzi*, ed. Paola Masino (Milan: Mondadori, 1961), 2:486.

Introduction

so strong as to live lives beyond those tied to their creators and, indeed, to "traverse thousands of forms and styles without losing their original force."[64] Futurism necessarily had been "avant-gardist and aristocratic," whereas Novecento would seek a relationship with the "people." Myths served this purpose, achieving a kind of universality, and so, in contrast to futurism's "pure" art, Novecento's would be "applied." Reaching the people, this art would have a function today and tomorrow. As the director of *Quadrante* in the early 30s, Bontempelli discussed with collaborator Carlo Belli the importance of isolating Novecento — both artistic and literary — from futurism. In the past, he had been a futurist, too, for "then there was nothing else." But times had changed: even Marinetti knew that futurism was going nowhere. Like *900* had cast off literary futurism, it was now important for *Quadrante* to make it clear that "the part of (artistic) Novecentism that we're against is precisely that part that's remained futurist."[65] In Bontempelli's eyes, recycling futurism — in mentality or technique — just wasn't groundbreaking anymore.

For many, futurism remains, at least philosophically speaking, the fascist art movement par excellence, its belligerence the quintessential expression of fascism's "apotheosis of war."[66] This renders Bontempelli's attempts to displace futurism from the fascist throne and place Novecento there in its stead one of the most striking aspects of his critical work. Bontempelli had agreed that futurism's strength was its destructive bent, but this was what, in his eyes, made it inadequate for the purposes of the regime, whose task it was to build anew. (In this, the regime's spirit was

---

64. This particular citation comes from one of the articles in which Bontempelli reiterated the differences between his movement and Marinetti's. It was published in the magazine *Futurism*, June 15, 1931 (n.p.), GRI 66, but the first major essay in which Bontempelli laid out the differences between Novecento and futurism was "Analogies," cited above.
65. Letter from Bontempelli to Carlo Belli, Frascati, December 12, 1935, MART Fondo Belli.
66. Walter Benjamin, epilogue to "The Work of Art in the Age of Mechanical Reproduction," in *Illuminations*, ed. Hannah Arendt (New York: Schocken, 1968), 241–42. For a response to this line of criticism, see Patricia Gaborik and Andrea Harris, "From Italy and Russia to France and the U.S.: 'Fascist' Futurism and Balanchine's 'American' Ballett," in *Avant-garde Performance and Material Exchange: Vectors of the Radical*, ed. Mike Sell (Basingstoke, UK: Palgrave Macmillan, 2011), 23–40.

Introduction

kindred to Novecento's, for the fascists imagined themselves not as liquidators of the avant-garde, but as revolutionaries in their own right. Scholars have in fact identified fascism as a form of political modernism that arose in tandem with the artistic ones.[67])

The philosophical aspects of the futurism-fascism-Novecento ménage are too complex to be adequately addressed here, nonetheless, the ways in which the two artistic movements positioned themselves with respect to Mussolini's regime are instructive. At times, their language was similar. If in 1920 the futurist ringleader suggested that art could offer spiritual but not material solace, writing that, "We won't have earthly paradise, but the economic inferno will be brightened up and pacified by innumerable artistic parties,"[68] Bontempelli seemed to imply something comparable when he said that the new art should "cover with smiles the saddest of things." In reality, as we have seen, he was ready to place Novecento in the regime's service, if not on a base propagandistic level, on a deeper, spiritual one. Marinetti sang a slightly different tune. While futurist manifestoes including the 1924 "Futurism and Fascism," pledged admiration for Mussolini's "futurist temperament" and support for the political party the movement had helped create, they also marked a separation between art and politics that was foreign to early futurism, essentially proclaiming the movement's non-interest in quotidian political action: "Futurism is an artistic and ideological movement. It intervenes in political battles only in moments of grave danger to the nation."[69] Bontempelli, conversely, would argue against any such distinction:

> If "fascism" were only the name of a party or a political preference (however victorious and flourishing), art would have nothing to do with it: they would be two

---

67. See for example Jeffrey T. Schnapp, "Forwarding Address," *Stanford Italian Review* 8.1–2 (1990): 53–80.
68. "Al di là del comunismo," in *Teoria e invenzione*, 424. On Marinetti's pessimism and shift away from politics, see Emilio Gentile, "'Il regno dell'uomo dalle radici tagliate': Disumanismo e anticristianesimo nella rivoluzione futurista (1909–1920)," in Gloria Manghetti, *Firenze Futurista, 1909–1920: Atti del convegno di studi, Firenze, 15–16 maggio 2009* (Florence: Polistampa, 2010), 143–76. On futurism and politics more generally, in English, Günter Berghaus, *Futurism and Politics: Between Anarchist Rebellion and Fascist Reaction, 1909–1944* (Providence, RI: Berghahn Books, 1996).
69. "Futurismo e fascismo," in Marinetti, *Teoria e invenzione*, 430.

independent and incommunicable worlds. But by "fascism" we mean a whole orientation of life, public and private: a total and perfected order that is practical and theoretical, intellectual and moral, application and spirit. We all agree on this (and those who don't simply don't count).[70]

And so, fascism had inaugurated the "third epoch of human civilization," and art was the "sensitive instrument that must at once mark off and foster, express and bring to maturation the fecundity" of that epoch.[71] The Bontempelli who had come round to futurism during WWI because he wanted to make "action-art" now, in 1926, posited that the Novecentists, not the futurists, had such desires. And such potential. His commitment to what he thought would be a revolution — spiritual, social, political, artistic — was what drove his anti-futurist stance. Bontempelli-Novecentist wasn't cowering in the face of avant-garde destruction, nor was he asphyxiated by the imposition of fascist order. He was, along with the regime, he thought, "striv[ing] to transform the catastrophe into a miracle," in the form of new myths for a modern age.[72]

Discovering Reality: Myth and Magic Realism

I'm telling of true events, which happened to me, in the city of Milan. This narrative — which contains the adventures that happened to me one afternoon, between 12 and 12:30, as I was going from Via San Paolo to the Galleria — could seem too complicated for all of those who are capable of going from home to a trattoria without encountering anything worth repeating. / And yet this is a true story.[73]

Thus begins the first of ten mini-novels comprising *The Intense Life*. Despite pre-dating Novecento's debut by seven years, it perfectly encapsulates the spirit of that movement, which, as we've seen, aimed to create new myths for the modern age and would employ magic realism to do so. The grounding of that spirit, as the passage

---

70. Schnapp, *Primer*, 218–20.
71. Ibid., 219–20.
72. Poggioli, *Theory*, 65.
73. *La vita intensa*, in *Opere scelte*, 7.

Introduction

suggests, was one of adventure. It's not a given that anything special happened to the narrator Massimo that day, only that he — perhaps unlike others — was capable of *seeing* something worth being told. The second half of the term "magic realism" shouldn't be forgotten, for the world Bontempelli crafted could seem decidedly real. His fictional cities, for instance, are made up of the exact same streets, landmarks and distances of their real-world counterparts, though the "daimôn" caveat still holds true.[74] As literary critic Carlo Bo, the writer's much younger contemporary, discerned, "in Bontempelli there was no desire to surpass the confines of reality. For him, reality was already a boundless realm of mysteries, problems, characters without keys."[75] Bomtempelli–narrator had a watchful eye or, as one critic called it, a "secret gaze," which, truth be told, even characters born before him had as well.[76] One of the most poignant examples is *Watching the Moon*'s Maria, who travels to the literal ends of the earth in an attempt to rescue her (dead) daughter, whom she believes has been kidnapped by the moon. This attitude wasn't reserved for Bontempelli's characters. The Novecentists themselves were to hold it, too: "The most everyday and normal we want to see as an adventurous miracle: continuous risk and continuous efforts of heroism or trickery to avoid it," their leader would write.[77] It was in their power to render reality magic.

The defining term he borrowed from German art critic Franz Roh, who had coined it in 1923 to categorize a new tendency in painting that had begun with such friends of Bontempelli as Carrà and De Chirico — those attached to the aforementioned *Valori plastici* that would champion the *rappel à l'ordre*. Through his *900* collaborator Georg Kaiser, Bontempelli was closely connected to German circles and therefore likely already had the term on his radar when, in 1924, Nino Frank would use it in an article about Bontempelli for a Belgian journal. Roh's book, *Nach Expressionismus: Magischer Realismus: Probleme der neuesten europäischen Malerei*

---

74. See page xiv.
75. Carlo Bo, preface to Bontempelli, *Racconti e romanzi*, 1: xv.
76. Giuseppe Amoroso, *Il realismo magico di Bontempelli* (Messina: La editrice universitaria, c. 1950–60), 13.
77. "Giustificazione," 19.

Introduction

(*Post-Expressionism: Magic Realism: Problem in the Newest European Painting*) was well-known in Italy.[78]

Bontempelli adopted the term, but attached it, rather than to Roh's objects of study, to the Italian artists of the *quattrocento* (the fifteenth century) — Massaccio, Mantegna, Piero della Francesca — who had in his view, more than his contemporaries, "so fully put into effect that 'magic realism' that we may assume as a definition of our tendency."[79] As he would explain and re-explain for years to come, with "magic" he had meant neither "witchcraft" nor "fantasy for the sake of fantasy — *Arabian Nights*," but, almost simply, imagination.[80] The "precise realism [...] wrapped in an atmosphere of lucid wonder" of *quattrocento* painting is what appealed to him:

> The more weight and solidity [the *quattrocento* painter] gave to his material, the more he wanted to tell us that his most intense love was for *some other thing* around or beyond it. [...] Herein lay that *wonder*, expression of magic, the true protagonist of fifteenth-century painting: herein lay those atmospheres *in tension*, even more precise and vibrant than the forms of the material represented.[81]

The "supernatural," or perhaps better, intensified nature emerges as an element of the Bontempellian fictional world, where nature provides a counterweight to the solidity of the matter — and often mechanized matter — of the modern materialist world depicted. Elements like air, water and sunshine fill the atmosphere with that "tension" he wrote of, acting sometimes as intangible but often visible forces that radically alter characters' lives. One of the most masterful examples is the sun-drenched reincarnation of a child in *The Boy with Two Mothers*, but a quintessential instance

---

78. Emily Braun, *Mario Sironi and Italian Modernism: Art and Politics under Fascism* (New York: Cambridge University Press, 2000); Elena Pontiggia, "Bontempelli e gli artisti," in Massimo Bontempelli, *Realismo Magico e altri scritti sull'arte,* ed. Elena Pontiggia (Milan: Abscondita, 2006), 123–57; Irene Guenther, "Magic Realism, New Objectivity, and the Arts during the Weimar Republic," in Lois Parkinson Zamora and Wendy B. Faris, *Magical Realism: Theory, History, and Community* (Durham, NC: Duke University Press, 1995), 60: Maggie Ann Bowers, *Magic(al) Realism* (London: Routledge, 2004; repr. 2005).
79. "Analogie," 36.
80. "Che cos'è il realismo magico?" 4.
81. "Analogie," 36.

Introduction

comes from the 1935 play in this volume, *Nembo* (*Stormcloud*), in which a horrible cloud arrives in a town, mysteriously killing its children.

As we know, Bontempelli tied Novecento, and by extension the practice of myth and magic realism, explicitly to his desire to create a literature for the fascist era. The correspondence between the two most explicitly emerges perhaps in his writing on the theater, where he auspicated a performance that would offer a sublime experience to the Italian masses, "a people who can easily breathe the sublime."[82] This performance — eminently theatrical — would through new myths, fables and characters create a primordial atmosphere that would in its turn inspire action, rather than allowing the public to sit as passive observers. Such theater didn't necessarily need to be held outdoors for large numbers, but Bontempelli did see the utility of a vast theater for celebratory and political ceremonies: "And who knows if it might be precisely from these that the germ of a new theatrical form can't be born." This sort of theater would recall that of his youth, at least how he, as an impassioned spectator, had experienced it: as a theater that "evoked and fed collective passions," acting as a force for spiritual assembly.[83]

Critics have quite willingly followed the head Novecentist in finding an ideal correspondence — ideological as well as methodological — between his movement and fascism. While judging the writer's attitude to be complex and finally ambivalent, one scholar has in fact argued that Bontempelli's suggestions for the theater were not at all extraneous to the "aestheticization of political life that fascism erected as the fulcrum of its surreptitiously unifying activity."[84] The "aestheticization of politics" formula is, of course, Walter Benjamin's and dates back to the seminal late-1930s essay, "The Work of Art in the Age of Mechanical Reproduction," where the German philosopher presented the aestheticization of politics as the fascist mode of mass domination, to which

---

82. "Il vecchio spettacolo, come la pensavo nel '28," 354.
83. "Teatro per le masse (conclusioni)," in "Il vecchio spettacolo, come la pensavo nel '32," in *AN*, 385, 378.
84. Carlo Cecchini is one of few scholars who has explored Bontempelli's fascism, from an aesthetic point of view, in depth: *Avanguardia mito ideologia: Massimo Bontempelli tra futurismo e fascismo* (Rome: Il ventaglio, 1986), 130.

Introduction

Communism responded by politicizing aesthetics. For Benjamin, a Marxist Jew who committed suicide during an escape attempt to avoid capture by the Nazis, the fascists' aestheticizing strategies allowed them to force the masses "to their knees," beguiling them into experiencing their "own destruction as an aesthetic pleasure of the first order"[85]: his was a fascism that, in the Bontempellian phrase by now familiar to the reader, "covered with smiles the saddest of things." Generations of scholars have followed in Benjamin's footsteps, analyzing fascism above all as a spectacular phenomenon and considering both the rallies held in Italian *piazze* and government-sponsored theatrical performances the tools for completing the regime's deceptive, destructive mission.

Equally significant for historians and culture critics is Bontempelli's recourse to myth and magic realism. His desire to recapture a primordial spirit aligned well with fascism's attempt to create a united community based on a mythic conception of the nation. For the late George Mosse, the "fascist myth was based upon the national mystique," in which even contrasting fragments of the past, like romanticism and socialism, were "integrated into a coherent attitude toward life." Mosse asserted that "'Magic realism' stood side by side with the romanticized view of the past that anchored fascist myth: whether it was the ancient Germans who had defeated the Roman legions or those Roman ruins that were now bathed mightily in romantic light [...]."[86] And, as Ruth Ben-Ghiat has shown, it was one of many realisms of interest in the fascist era able to "'transfigure' reality rather than represent it."[87]

Still, Bontempelli worked to add complexity and layers of truth, not merely to wash truth away, as he so eloquently explained to actor Lamberto Picasso, who staged *Valòria, ovvero la famiglia del fabbro* (*Valòria, or the Blacksmith's Family*, 1932). Bontempelli would consider the performance a success if people enjoyed it,

---

85. Benjamin, "The Work of Art in the Age of Mechanical Reproduction," 242.
86. George L. Mosse, *The Fascist Revolution: Toward a General Theory of Fascism* (New York: Howard Fertig, 1999), 23–25. For a view on magic realism as mediation, see Keala Jewell, "Magic Realism and Real Politics: Massimo Bontempelli's Literary Compromise," *Modernism/Modernity* 15.4 (2008): 725–44.
87. Ben-Ghiat, *Fascist Modernities*, 50. See also Roger Griffin, *Modernism and Fascism: The Sense of a Beginning under Mussolini and Hitler* (Basingstoke, UK: Palgrave Macmillan, 2007).

laughed more than once, found it euphoric — and on the way home kept thinking about it, realizing only then that the play had a terribly cruel pathos about it.[88] It's important, therefore, to avoid distilling Bontempelli's production down to something that worked as fascist literature because it romanticized, or papered over, the harsh realities of life. A great admirer of Bontempelli's writing, il Duce himself had seen that the source of truth in *Vita e morta di Adria e dei suoi figli* (*Life and Death of Adria and Her Children*, 1929) was the very "unreality" of its plot.[89]

The complexity of such questions can't be satisfyingly addressed in these few pages, but the story told here is valuable as a check on the impulse to imagine facile and monolithic correspondences between a particular aesthetic and a particular politics. Mussolini preferred a pluralistic arts policy, but this isn't the only reason that neither futurism nor Novecento — nor any other movement — came to officially represent the regime. Finding a perfect one-to-one ideological correspondence would have been no easy feat, for neither the art movements nor fascism were so uniform as to make that possible. No less significantly, as Emilio Gentile has reminded us, to conceive of fascism itself as something that existed in a "pure" ideological state is in itself erroneous, not only because fascism itself changed over time — the fascism of 1919 was quite different from that of 1924 or '37 or '44 — but because what defined it was not a timeless, innate mode of thought, but the functioning of its institutions and individuals over the twenty years of its reign.[90] To accept a binary like Walter Benjamin's is in fact a historically complicated task: or, better, a task complicated by a history that shows that the fascists weren't (aren't) the only to aestheticize politics and, likewise, that the Italian fascists were as apt to politicize aesthetics as their Soviet contemporaries or anyone else.[91]

As the polemics over Novecento indicate, there were several competing and even contradictory ideas about what it would mean to create a fascist art — or even to think or act "like a fascist."

---

88. Note to *Valòria*, in Bontempelli, *Teatro*, 2:77.
89. Letter from Lando Ferretti (head of Mussolini's press office) to Bontempelli, in Cigliana, "Due epistolari," 82.
90. Emilio Gentile, introduction to the updated (1996) edition of *Le origini dell'ideologia fascista 1918–1925*, 23.
91. *Ibid.*, 27: Russel A. Berman, "The Aestheticization of Politics: Walter Benjamin on Fascism and the Avant-Garde," *Stanford Italian Review* 8.1–2 (1990): 35–52.

Introduction

In the world of the theater alone, the proposals were countless. Gabriele D'Annunzio reminded Mussolini that the best of fascism had been generated by his spirit. The futurists rejected D'Annunzio as sentimental and decadent and then claimed the same thing. Bontempelli then did a different version of this. Pirandello's plays were at the center of debate, as some found them too meditative and dark to be fascist, whereas Mussolini said they were wonderfully fascist "without even wanting" to be: they taught that the world was what you wished to make it. Pirandello agreed with him.[92] When it came to myth and magic realism, too, Bontempelli may not have articulated in manifesto form the quintessence of his art until 1926, but his practice of it both predated and outlasted fascism — fascism as a movement and his own faith in it (again, magic didn't disappear from his works even once he had begrudged the formula). What's more, a figure like Savinio — no fascist, but a great believer in the use of myth on the stage — complicates the tendency to identify a supposedly inherent fascism of a philosophy, or an aesthetic, or a method of communication, as does the fact that great leftist thinkers like Georges Sorel and Antonio Gramsci[93] had emphasized the importance of myth in the creation of communities.

These are just some of the reasons it seems less useful to think about "intrinsic fascism" than to reflect instead on the myriad of ways that cultural roots and experiences — the impact of modernization and the war, developments in science and technology, the rise of capitalist consumer culture, new explorations in philosophy — converged to create a variety of modernisms that included not just artistic movements like futurism and Novecento (and expressionism, surrealism, etc.) but political ones, such as

---

92. On D'Annunzio's and Pirandello's theater in relation to fascism, Mary Ann Frese Witt, *The Search for Modern Tragedy: Aesthetic Fascism in Italy and France* (Ithaca: Cornell University Press, 2001).
93. Georges Sorel (1847–1922) was a French political writer; a socialist and theorist of revolutionary syndicalism, he was an important influence on the young, socialist Mussolini. Antonio Gramsci (1831–1937) was one of the twentieth century's most important Marxist philosophers and secretary of the Italian Communist Party. He was imprisoned by the fascist government in 1926 and had yet to gain his freedom when, extremely ill, he died in a clinic in 1937. Among his most important writings on political theory and Italian history and culture are those he composed while incarcerated, published as the *Prison Notebooks*.

fascism, too. Similarly, while boxing our discourse about the fascist era in the theoretical language and logic of inherency often leaves us trapped, our muscles cramped, re-examining the historical record, looking at cases like Bontempelli's, seeking out the moments that trouble this discourse and not just those that confirm it, enables us to kick the box wide open, and in the process, learn not just about the writer but about fascism, too.

It becomes difficult to see myth or magic realism, for instance, in perfect, symbiotic union with fascism when we think about its international success throughout the rest of the twentieth century and, indeed, into the twenty-first. Fredric Jameson's commentary on late Soviet magic realism and the way capitalism figures as the "mysterious unknowable outside power" in Alexander Sokurov's 1988 film *Days of Eclipse* would provide one point of comparison here, as the spiritual void Bontempelli combatted was created as much by the rise of consumer capitalism in the early twentieth century as by the war or the avant-garde.[94]

Bontempelli's magic realism wasn't the magic realism of the Americas, either, but the sorts of things that have caused scholars to see magic realism as a strong right arm for fascism — including its mythic and romantic construction of a place or a community — are aspects of both Bontempelli's European method and its American descendants, whose authors were often engaged on the left, as socialists or communists.

In some recent studies, the Italian author's importance in a genealogy of magic realism has been acknowledged, though it is a question worthy of much further reflection. Of course, it is the "magical realism" of Latin American literature that has become most renowned, and the paths by which Bontempelli arrived there, on page, stage and in person, were many. *Nostra Dea* was quickly translated after its 1925 premiere, and Bontempelli's fiction debuted in Ortega y Gasset's journal, *Revista de Occidente,* in 1926.[95] In the 1930s, in Mexico, Bontempelli was promoted by poet and playwright Xavier Villaurrutia, who, after studying at Yale, returned to his native country and founded its first experimental

---

94. Frederic Jameson, *The Geopolitical Aesthetic: Cinema and Space in the World System* (Bloomington: Indiana University Press, 2005), 111.
95. Roh's book would be published by *Revista* the next year: *Realismo mágico Post expresionismo: Problemas de la pintura europea más reciente.* (Madrid: Revista de Occidente, 1927).

Introduction

theater: Villaurrutia translated and directed *Minnie la candida* in 1938. Bontempelli's visit to Buenos Aires, with Pirandello, in 1933 was an important one for disseminating his ideas. He gave several talks, one of which was entirely dedicated to literary Novecento and, under that umbrella, magic realism.[96] Finally, perhaps most important are those cohabitations in 1920s–30s Paris. The Cuban revolutionary and writer Alejo Carpentier, one of the first practitioners of Latin American magical realism, though he called his own method *lo real maravilloso*, arrived as a voluntary exile to the city in 1928 (thus during the *900* years), where Bontempelli's friend, Venezuelan writer Arturo Uslar-Pietri, in turn befriended him. In 1948, Uslar-Pietri was the first to apply the concept of magic realism to Latin American fiction.[97] Bontempelli's enduring presence in the Southern Americas is attested to by more recent creations: Chilean director Raul Ruiz's 2000 film *The Comedy of Innocence* was adapted from *The Boy with Two Mothers*.

Carpentier and his descendants in the Americas have diverged from Bontempelli's path in important ways, however, even if some similarities in their approach exist. As Bontempelli painted futurism as destructive in an effort to tout the reconstructive qualities of the new Novecento myths, in *The Kingdom of This World*, Carpentier distanced himself from the Europeans who had inspired him. He did this mainly by exaggeratedly stressing that European surrealism offered a "marvelous invoked in disbelief" — as a mere literary experiment — while his marvelous real was something encountered daily in the Americas.[98] Literature of the *real maravilloso*, for Carpentier, was the expression of an alternate, uniquely American reality, in fact "the heritage of all of America." Accordingly, as he wrote in his preface, his story was rigorously true in its recounting of "extraordinary events" that

---

96. The texts of those talks, as then reported in the Buenos Aires newspaper, *Il Mattino d'Italia*, can be read in *L'Illuminista* 5.13–15 (2005): 195–224.
97. On these relationships and also on the importance of "primitivism" in Paris at the time and later in Latin American magical realism, see Erik Camayd-Freixas, "Reflections on Magical Realism: A Return to Legitimacy, the Legitimacy of Return," *Canadian Review of Comparative Literature* 23 (June 1996): 581–89.
98. An extended but slightly different version of Carpentier's original preface can be found in Zamora and Faris, *Magical Realism*, 76–88.

would simply be "impossible to situate in Europe."[99] As Carpentier saw it, his European forebears engaged in a sort of sterile aesthetic pretense, while he was more like a prophet of a sort of American exceptionalism.

Additionally, Carpentier's insistence on events, rather than on a particular gaze, marks his departure from a Bontempellian sort of magic realism. As a matter of fact, one way critics have distinguished magic realism (*à la* Bontempelli) from magical or marvelous realism (*à la* Carpentier or Garcia Marquez) is to specify that the "magic" in the former refers to "the mystery of life" and in the latter to "any extraordinary occurrence and particularly to anything spiritual or unaccountable by rational science."[100] This is only in part a fair distinction, as Bontempelli's stories — the foundational magic realist texts — are full of extraordinary and unexplainable events, too: a boy's reincarnation *(The Boy with Two Mothers)*, a young girl's dissolution into the waters of a brook *(Water)*, café customers feeling a sudden malaise, not knowing it emanates from the stare of a hateful woman at a table nearby *(Sunday)*. The truth is that most scholars have named Bontempelli *en passant* as a founding father but haven't dedicated much time to actually analyzing his works; doing so would far advance the conversation in this area of study.

The real distinction between Bontempelli and his more contemporary American heirs is to be found not in the absence or presence of extraordinary events, then, but in the capacity to view an event — any event — with the "secret gaze."[101] Indeed, as discussed above, in *The Intense Life* the narrator Massimo stresses that his tale is true, much like Carpentier did later in *Kingdom*. What made those events extraordinary was Bontempelli's capacity to *see* in them something *worth being told*. This gaze was but one of the ways that Bontempelli's magic realism was completely devoid of, even contrary to, the "particularism" of Carpentier. A Bontempellian magic moment could happen anywhere, such was the cosmopolitanism — and universalism — of his outlook: his

---

99. Translated from its preface, in the Italian, in Alejo Carpentier, *Il regno di questo mondo* (Torino: Einaudi, 1990), xi; this passage does not appear in the Zamora and Faris translation.
100. Bowers, *Magic(al) Realism*, 20.
101. See p. xxxvii above.

Introduction

interest lay in the creation of new myths for a modern age, not in creating a world apart.

MASSIMO AND LUIGI, BEYOND *PIRANDELLISMO*

Luigi Pirandello is one of those literary legends so influential as to have given his name not just to an adjective — Pirandellian — but even to a noun: *Pirandellismo*. The Sicilian novelist and playwright was the master, on narrative page and theatrical stage alike, of the identity crisis. In *Uno, Nessuno e Centomila (One, No One, and One Hundred Thousand,* 1926), Moscardo is thrown into despair when his wife tells him his nose tilts to the right, which he had never realized before. In *Così è (se vi pare) (Right you are (if you think so),* 1917), a entire village goes into a tizzy when Signor Ponza, his mother-in-law Signora Frola, and a third woman arrive, for no one knows if this third woman is Ponza's first wife and Frola's daughter or his second wife, whom Frola, driven mad by her daughter's death, only imagines is her child. Finally, in the landmark 1921 *Sei personaggi in cerca d'autore (Six Characters in Search of an Author),* these troubled creatures come looking for someone who can complete their unfinished story. When a theatrical director takes them on, trouble begins: how can they be sure that the performance will show them as they "really" are, as they each imagine themselves to be? Thus "Pirandellian" has come to refer to stories where conflicts emerge between an individual's sense of self and others' perception of that self, and, especially, where truth is at best relative, at worst unknowable. *Pirandellismo* is the practice of writing such stories and an activity in which numerous Italian authors of the period, including Bontempelli, are said to have engaged. Because Pirandello has remained *the* voice of that generation — and rightly so, for plays like *Six Characters* were truly revolutionary — it's unfortunately been too easy to speak of an entire cluster of playwrights as those who merely produced lesser examples of *Pirandellismo*.

Although especially as a novelist Bontempelli earned an important stature of his own — younger "Bontempellians" weren't unheard of — his theater has often been seen in this light. This isn't entirely without reason, for he, too, was intrigued by the dissolution of subjectivity in modern, bourgeois society and also tackled questions of identity's fixedness, or lack thereof. It is entirely possible to fit plays like *Nostra Dea* and *Valòria* into a Pirandellian realm. In the first, Dea's personality is wholly dependent on the clothing she wears: in her slip, she is listless, barely moving or speaking; in a red tailored suit, she is strong and lively; in a green serpentine gown, she acts like a viper, and speaks like one, too, with a sibilant "s." One of the questions that emerges in the play, then, is, "who is Dea, really?" and certainly, that the piece had its triumphant premier under the Sicilian maestro's direction and as part of his Teatro d'Arte repertoire has only reinforced the sense of it as having even been inspired by him. In *Valòria*, Eteocle the Blacksmith (called Teo) has been acquitted of a murder due to lack of sufficient evidence. The townsfolk are pretty sure he did it, but he's a likable guy, so they celebrate his release. When Eteocle discovers, however, that he's not perceived as truly innocent, he demands a retrial, locking himself and his family in the courtroom cell until he can prove his innocence to one and all. But this resolution is withheld.

Bontempelli scholars are in essential agreement: it's not unfair to speak of a Pirandellian influence on him; but the reverse is also true. Theirs was a relationship of mutual exchange and, indeed, osmosis. Instances of Bontempelli's *Pirandellismo*, in other words, can be listed alongside examples of Pirandello's *Bontempellismo*. Worth particular mention in this regard is the Sicilian playwright's move toward myth in the wake of Bontempelli's call for new myths for the modern age. Their mutual exchange was based in no small part on the fact that the two men were close friends. Born in 1867, Pirandello was eleven years Bontempelli's senior, but by the time they became acquaintances in the early twentieth century, both were mature adults with careers set in motion — both had also passed through unsatisfying years teaching, only to abandon that trade for the pen. Already in 1910 Pirandello proposed they use the familiar form of address — "Yes, come on. Let's use the 'tu,' if it pleases you as it pleases me."[102] — and wrote to his friend of the sadness that would plague him until the end of his days. Over the years they spent a great deal of time together when they were in the same city and shared numerous experiences: the founding of the Teatro d'Arte, membership in the Royal Academy, travel together, especially the South American tour where both acted as cultural

---

102. Letter from Luigi Pirandello to Bontempelli, July 22, 1910, GRI 9, 24.

emissaries for the regime. The closeness of their relationship is intimated by the sorrow and guilt both Bontempelli and Paola Masino felt when Pirandello passed away. Had they not gone to Florence and left him "alone" in Rome at a difficult time — in 1936, when his young love Marta Abba went to the U.S. to act on Broadway — maybe he wouldn't have died. This was a sentiment that Masino wrote of in her diary, and Bontempelli admitted in his commemoration of the dear departed, *Pirandello, o del candore*.[103]

Still, rather than rehearsing the tally of each writer's influence on the other, focusing on whether Pirandello's work can be considered magic realism or where Bontempelli's plays become most Pirandellian, it seems fresher to give space to the commonalities in their work that go beyond labels like *Pirandellismo*. Shifting the discussion away from influence and toward commonality, in fact, is in and of itself productive. The very notion of influence leaves something to be desired, for it can coax us to imagine the two men working together in a bubble, giving or taking from one another but from no one or nothing else. This obviously isn't true, and in their epoch, certain themes — like the instability of identity — or types of characters — like automata — proliferated, not because one writer thought them up and the rest rode his coattails, but because these were the apprehensions of the day that many artists grappled with in their own, more or less unique and original, ways.

One source of angst in "the Age of Pirandello," as one monograph dubbed it, was the rise of mass society. Fiercely antidemocratic both, in such works as *La Sagra del Signore della nave* (*The Festival of Our Lord of the Ship*) and *Valòria*, Pirandello and Bontempelli, respectively, revealed themselves to be no less concerned about the threatening power of the democratized masses than the likes of sociologist Gustave Le Bon, who had published *The Crowd: A Study of the Popular Mind* in 1895,[104] or one of his most notorious disciples, Benito Mussolini.

We have already seen that both Pirandello and Bontempelli took to task a bourgeois milieu that created traumas both metaphysical and social for the individual. But, as Bontempelli observed in his brilliant eulogy, the maestro's characters' plight wasn't — as in Ibsen — a battle against others, but a desperate desire to live in communion with them, as individuals one and all. *Festival* and

---

103. Bontempelli, "Pirandello o del candore," in *Opere scelte*, 809–28.
104. Gustave Le Bon, *Psychologie des foules* (Paris: F. Alcan, 1895).

Introduction

Valòria both reveal in acute, eminently theatrical ways, that such concerns weren't about abstract notions of society or even the behavior of particular individuals, but instead, that overwhelming power of the people brought together and transformed into what Bontempelli described as a frightening mass with a "blind force."[105]

The representation and management of crowds in performance was hardly a new phenomenon when the two playwrights began to concern themselves with it. Already in the last quarter of the previous century, Georg II, duke of Saxe-Meinengen, had impressed crowds across Europe with his artful manipulation of the masses on stage, and in Italy the opera had long required vast numbers of singers to be present in the choruses. There had been D'Annunzio, too, whose plays, including *La Gloria* (*Glory*, 1899) and *La figlia di Jorio* (*Jorio's Daughter*, 1904), entailed orchestrating the chanting multitudes whose presence was anything but negligible in the unfolding of the action. The author of *Six Characters* followed in D'Annunzio's footsteps: when *Festival* premiered — the maestro selected it to inaugurate his Teatro d'Arte — his skillful organization of 120 extras astonished the spectating public but was truly important precisely because it was the fulcrum of the piece's analysis of crowd behavior. The same would be true of *Valòria* when it appeared almost a decade later. That play's *Pirandellismo* — one of the reasons for which it has been unfairly dismissed — is quite effective, but the real interest of the piece lies in its depiction of the masses' power.[106]

The festival that gives Pirandello's play its name unfolds in a piazza in front of a little church. On the same early September Sunday that hosts the season's first pig slaughter, villagers come from far and wide to celebrate the Lord, who once rescued their fishermen from a terrible shipwreck. And so those 120 actors represented the array of humanity brought together: revelers on

---

105. "Pirandello o del candore," 816–19.
106. Fulvia Airoldi Namer notes that Bontempelli's novel *La famiglia del fabbro* (*The Blacksmith's Family*, 1932) is Pirandellian, and that Pirandello's *Festival* may have influenced the transformation of it into the play *Valòria, La famiglia del fabbro* (*Valòria, or the Blacksmith's Family*), though she doesn't indicate the aspects that lead her to link the two pieces. See *Massimo Bontempelli* (Milan: Mursia, 1979), 154. Elsewhere in the book — a monograph with several interesting points of interpretation of Bontempelli's opus — she discusses his interest in the masses and mass spectacle, though not in conjunction with this work.

Introduction

one hand, worshippers on the other, creating an intensely violent "contrast between bestial carnality and the longing of the spirit," as D'Amico argued in his review.[107] Signor Lavaccara, distraught when the family's pig, Nicola, goes to slaughter, debates with a Young Pedagogue if man is superior to the beast he butchers. The Pedagogue begins as mankind's champion, but as the party goes on and the crowd degenerates into an "obscene and frightening spectacle of triumphant bestiality," he cries, "They are drunk, they've gone mad, but look at them crying for their bloodied Christ! And you want a tragedy more tragedy than this?"[108] The play was, as its author had written in his program note, a picture of people coming together and "becoming ugly" — for anti-Mussolinians like reviewer Corrado Alvaro a condemnation of those coming to the *piazza* in search of a false god; for those attuned to the anti-democratic impulses of the day, one that suggested the masses would be beastly until someone tamed them.[109]

Festival's folkloric aspect risks distracting the reader — less so a potential viewer, if the play were to be resurrected — from its very modern, potentially phantasmagoric effect.[110] The piece is wonderfully theatrical, especially in the finale, which sees the crowd process with a statue of Christ through the house and into the theater's foyer (like the Six Characters whose shattering of the fourth wall remains the theater's most iconic). This theatricality, and in particular the spectacularity lent to the play by the mass itself, is its foremost quality: the same that returns in Bontempelli's *Valòria*. It's a shame that play hasn't been given due attention — in accordance with Baldacci's pitting of a good (avant-garde) Bontempelli of the 1920s against a bad (conciliatory, return to order) Bontempelli

---

107. Silvio D'Amico, "Il Teatro d'arte di Pirandello," in Silvio D'Amico, *Cronache 1914/1955*. (Palermo: Novecento, 2002), 2.2:487.
108. Luigi Pirandello, *La Sagra del Signore della Nave*, in *La Sagra del Signore della Nave, L'Altro Figlio, La Giara: Commedie in un atto* (Florence: R. Bemporad & Figlio, 1925), 46, 50.
109. Alessandro D'Amico and Alessandro Tinterri, *Pirandello capocomico* (Palermo: Sellerio, 1987), 73. On the premier and its significance in terms of fascist politics and Pirandello's relationship with Mussolini, see Patricia Gaborik, "C'era Mussolini," in *Atlante*, 3:533–40. For additional reflections on fascist sponsorship of the theater, especially mass and popular spectacle, see my "Lo spettacolo del fascismo," in *Atlante*, 3:589–613.
110. Ferdinando Taviani makes acute observations in this regard in his *Uomini di scena uomini di libro: La scena sulla coscienza* (Bologna: Il Mulino, 1995; Rome: Officina Edizioni, 2010), 85–89.

Introduction

of the 1930s — for if sometimes Pirandello's plays suffer because their philosophical questions are rendered even more explicit than dramatically necessary, or compelling, *Valòria* avoids this pitfall not only where its Pirandellian themes are concerned but also in its pondering of the masses. On those counts, Bontempelli largely lets the theatricality do the talking: Teo's imprisonment in his fear of being wrongly judged by the others is rendered visually — but also subtly and comically — by his choice to lock himself in the cell. That the problem is finally his own is further underscored by the fact that, as the town blacksmith, he's the main person capable of forging or breaking the locks that would imprison him.

The play's dialogue is essentially reticent on the question of the masses. Here it is the sheer force of the bodies on stage and their driving of the action that unveil the theme. The pressures enacted by the townspeople on Teo and his family — made literal, physical — increase throughout and finally determine the play's outcome. The crowd's chaotic pulsion becomes particularly significant once Teo realizes that many think he is guilty and begins to search for a resolution. At a restaurant, where every attempt to go home is thwarted by the people wanting to celebrate with him, he learns that a brawl broke out on the street where the murder took place. One group wants the name changed to "Blacksmith Way," the other thinks it should be dedicated to the victim, "Poor Gaspar." When the town clerk says that a wreath has been placed at the scene of the crime, everyone wants Teo to go there and give a speech. He refuses, but the crowd overpowers and, as the scene comes to end, pushes Teo and his family off in that direction, singing the refrain that will provide the play's soundtrack through to its conclusion, "We will never know, know we never will…" — here in reference to who placed the wreath, but in general as regards Teo's presumed guilt.

In the final act, the blacksmith's attempts to have himself retried are first foiled by the judge and town officials' refusal to participate — despite the fact that the people filling the courtroom to the brim literally push them, like an ocean wave, into the jury box. Then, he's nearly satisfied by the villagers who decide to make themselves the jury. But, ultimately, his hopes dissolve when another fight breaks out, and after the excitement, the crowd loses interest in listening to the testimony, which for them is all for fun anyway. The disillusioned blacksmith wails that "Justice won't cheat him,"

Introduction

but the mass repeats their refrain: "We'll never know!" If the actions of the crowd don't actually supercede the rule of law — the initial judgment of the court stands — their sheer physical force threatens to become the rule of the agitated many. Both *The Festival of Our Lord of the Ship* and *Valòria, or the Blacksmith's Family* put into fantastic theatrical action the anxiety of the age of mass society, and mass politics. This was yet another area — and a highly significant one — where Bontempelli and Pirandello, two illustrious writers, and two great friends, found themselves in communion and found striking and distinctive ways to express themselves in dramatic form.

The younger of the two, however, identified in his friend and his works the quality he prized above all and sought most frequently to explore in his own literature: *candore*. There is no adequate translation for this term, and especially Bontempelli's use of it: "candor" conveys only the sense of frankness or sincerity. (The same is true for the adjective or noun applied to the person who possesses *candore*: the masculine *candido* or feminine *candida*, which isn't fully rendered by "candid.") In *candore*, sincerity is the natural result of an innocence or naivety, which, while they may contain an ounce of gullibility, don't at all imply a dullness or stupidity. On the contrary, as Bontempelli would describe, the person with *candore* possessed an elementary intelligence, where we should understand elementary as elemental, even primordial.[111] Let's turn to what Bontempelli said about his *candido* friend in *Pirandello, o del candore*, for the full explanation of a word that here I will leave in its original form.

Candore was what defined Pirandello as a person. It was a purity, a simplicity of custom, an easy naturalness that made it impossible to "accept others' judgments and make them his own." The *candida* soul saw the world in its own way — here it's easy to recall the Pirandello play, *Each in His Own Way* — and was never rocked by others' ways of seeing. The *candido*'s language was simple

---

111. "Pirandello, o del candore," 809–28. Translators Jack Street and Rod Umlas chose "genuine" in their translation of *Minnie la candida* (*Genuine Minnie*), a good solution for an essentially untranslatable term, even if it also leaves some aspects of the concept unrepresented. See Jack D. Street and Rod Umlas, *The Italian Theater of the Grotesque: A New Theater for the Twentieth Century. An Anthology* (Lewiston, NY: Edwin Mellen Press, 2003), 281–320.

Introduction

and elementary, and others' judgments he would often perceive as "complicated words." The furthest thing from hypocrisy, *candore* led its possessor to shun all ceremoniousness and formality, all conventions and "decorations." "The immediate effect of *candore* is sincerity. The *candida* soul makes no concessions. With its style and its sincerity, the *candida* soul, which is an elemental force, gets easily to the root of things" and so effortlessly identifies that which is convention and that which is elementary. Last but not least, "The *candida* soul is divinely imprudent."

For Bontempelli, *candore* was the key to understanding his friend's labor, the very thing that generated his "way of imagining and expressing himself." In fact, it was the very concept of *candore* that could clarify many questions about Pirandello's work, remedying equivocations that had emerged: he wasn't dark, the pessimist or nihilist others had accused of him being, nor was he — and this issue Bontempelli addressed explicitly in his talk — a "complicator." No: *candore* led one to see extreme consequences, and Pirandello's art was an art of "denunciation," it gave the gift of awareness, knowledge (*conoscenza*). With this knowledge, in works that always began with an act of audacity, Pirandello offered a blank slate. He made it possible for rebuilding to begin, which could only happen if one looked honestly at the world. It was the clear vision of the *candido* Pirandello that enabled a new beginning.

So, then, in January of 1937, around a month after Pirandello's death, Bontempelli implicitly crowned him an avant-gardist, saying that he sent the Second Epoch to its grave. Telling of the next novel Pirandello had planned to write, *Adam and Eve*, Bontempelli described a pre-*Endgame*: the couple find themselves, after a cataclysm, in a depopulated world. They were an Adam and Eve with the story of humanity behind, not before, them, who had the task of engendering a new race, once again. All of the maestro's work, Bontempelli proclaimed, had merely been the prelude to this one, which sadly would never come into being. It was "the preparation of the regenerative cataclysm." We've heard this language before, of course, and know where Bontempelli fit himself into the scheme of things. He would've been Adam and Eve's partner, working on that regeneration. As we shall see, Bontempelli put at the center of his work that *candido* — more often the *candida*, actually — whom he identified with the person, and the works, of Luigi Pirandello. Certainly from Bontempelli's perspective, this was the greatest kinship they shared, for there's good reason to think, he saw *candore* not just in his friend but in himself as well.

Bontempelli's Theater, or on *Candore*

Bontempelli's pronouncements against the theater abound: "It doesn't take great ability to say that theater's done for" (1924); "There is no public need nourishing the theater," and "The theater is a history concluded, finished [...] for the literati, there's nothing to do in the theater" (1926); "Let's pitch the prose theater, too" (1928).[112] On one hand, this is hardly surprising, for we know that Bontempelli was the master of renunciation. It's Bontempellian, we might say, to write one of the decade's greatest plays and then declare the theater defunct. On the other hand, this wasn't like the time he repudiated his Carduccian works and then ceased to write poetry. No: he kept writing plays throughout his career. Indeed, nowhere more than in his relationship with the dramatic arts do we see the writer's hope that what his high priest, a character in "Viaggio d'Europa," said was true: "To die is always to be reborn."[113] Nowhere more than in his plays do we see such a variety of forms and in this a real struggle to find a unique theatrical voice.[114]

The language of death pervades Bontempelli's theatrical treatises, too — and packs a certain punch when he celebrates director Anton Giulio Bragaglia's productions as the "funerals of the prose theater."[115] Killing the prose theater was a good thing, of course. Like the other futurists who created a *tabula rasa* upon which new literature could be written, Bragaglia's tiny underground lair, which hosted the newest experiments in Roman performance throughout the twenties, was the launching pad for something new. From the ashes of the old stages, new ones could arise, and this is

---

112. "Il vecchio spettacolo" in *AN*, 335–77.
113. Bontempelli, "Viaggio d'Europa" ("Europe's Voyage"), in *Opere Scelte*, 450–93.
114. Recent studies of Bontempelli's theater are scarce. The present volume is the fullest available in English. In Italian, see Luca Somigli's overview of the works and criticism: "Bontempelli drammaturgo: Un profile critico e biografico," *Bollettino '900* 1–2 (2010) at http://www3.unibo.it/boll900/numeri/2010-i/Somigli.html, accessed 15 July 2013.
115. "Giusto giudizio su Bragaglia ovvero i funerali del teatro di prosa," in *AN*, 353.

Introduction

what Bontempelli was after, explaining in 1936 when a volume of his drama was released, "I have a strange aversion for the theater. Perhaps my theater was born from that aversion."[116] He was an optimist, in 1928 arguing that the epoch was still young and, therefore, simply hadn't *yet* produced the performance that would become emblematic of it, but there was hope that "in the lengthy and splendid funerals of the long dead performance, the seed and the move toward the performance of the future is to be found."[117]

Accordingly, already in the twenties, Bontempelli championed trends toward the theatrical and spectacular, and in the thirties, as we've seen, mass theater projects. Like Bragaglia, he thought that the literati had failed the theater because they were too, well, literary. Anyone writing plays had to realize that his responsibility was toward the stage, not the page: he was a "preparer of shows."[118] (This didn't mean spectacle for the sake of spectacle, but the creation of works whose meaning lay in enactment rather than just recounting.) The chief defect of Bontempelli's theater is its tendency to intellectualize in sometimes abstract dialogue; however, his attention to theatricality was absolute. He sought to write easily-spoken lines — even when their content was strange. The stage sets he imagined were striking and often described with very particular details. The movement and action of his plays were not centered on, or dependent on, conversation — a fault of much theater written by novelists. We ought not to forget, though, that this attention to *mise-en-scene* came from a fundamentally agonistic stance toward the reigning commercial theater of the day. It was this discontent that drove Bontempelli-dramatist, just as it drove the Novecento author-critic.

That this agonism was accompanied by a diverted gaze and adventurous spirit —these were what made Bontempelli one of Calvino's[119] favorite writers — is proven by the recurring

---

116. *AN*, 377: also in Bontempelli's introduction to *Teatro*, 2:9–11.
117. "Inaugurazione del 'Teatro reale dell'opera' ovvero i funerali del melodramma," in *AN*, 353.
118. "Caducità del teatro," in *AN*, 346.
119. A member of the anti-fascist resistance during the Second World War, Italo Calvino (1923–85) was one of Italy's most successful twentieth-century authors. Highly esteemed abroad as well, Calvino is best remembered for his fables and fantastic literature, including such works as *The Baron in the Trees* and *The Nonexistent Knight*, as well as the postmodern novels *Invisible Cities* and *If On a Winter's Night a Traveler*.

Introduction

appearance of the *candida* in Bontempelli's theatrical pieces. The figure of the *candida* is far from isolated to the drama or to representations in female form. The terms *candido/a* and *candore* appear throughout his stories to designate innocence, spontaneity and the other qualities already discussed. And it's clear, given his attribution of the trait to Pirandello, that Bontempelli didn't see *candore* as a female characteristic. But he had a particular fascination for female characters, and he was keenly attuned to the fragility and naivety *candore* evoked. There's a possibility, therefore, that, given prevailing gender codes, *candore* was easily linked to the women Bontempelli saw as particularly vulnerable in the modern, bourgeois epoch (Dea and Adria, a woman who locks herself away from sight when age threatens to mar her exquisite beauty, are prime examples of this thinking).

On the other hand, the close tie of *candore* to the Novecento spirit of adventure — to an almost visionary comportment — is particularly well revealed in the plays translated here, *Watching the Moon* (1916), *Stormcloud* (1935) and *Cinderella* (1942), and their female protagonists. Something special emerges from Maria, Regina and Cinderella: their fearlessness, anchored by the *candida*'s certainty in her own beliefs. The delightful combination of naivety, hard-headedness and thirst for adventure — especially where Maria and Cinderella are concerned — results in a "radical, subversive strength," yielding a slate of strong and complex female characters, still sometimes a rare commodity on the stage.[120]

When Maria's baby dies in *Watching the Moon*, she cannot accept the truth. Some nuns looking after her take the dead baby away, and Maria finds the empty cradle bathed in the moonlight streaming through the window. She is convinced that the moon has kidnapped her child: that same moon who made Maria fall in love with the father, assuring that a child would be born. The moon makes her light from the babies she kidnaps, the distraught mother reasons, and so embarks on a journey to find the point where the moonlight enters the earth, to prevent the rays from reaching the earth's surface — and therefore from

---

120. This is a judgment of Luigi Fontanella, in a reference to Madina, the protagonist of *Water*, that is also appropriate to the *candide* discussed here. See his preface to Bontempelli, *The Faithful Lover*, trans. Estelle Gilson (Austin, TX: Host Publications, 2007), iv.

Introduction

engendering unions that in turn engender babies who will only fall victim to the moon's machinations.

As indicated, the 1916 text was a densely layered response to the avant-gardism of the era, and critics have readily seen it as a staging of the futurists' call to destroy symbolism's "romantic sentimentalism drenched with moonshine." A futurist vein can be found also in the "synthetic" quality of the short episodes and in moments of anti-romanticism, such as Maria's refusal to enter into conversation with a suicidal adolescent who would find his salvation in her. The play has a clearly expressionist feel as well, in its dreamlike episodic structuring of a journey and in characters who are more often types than fleshed-out persons. Some scenes pose a challenge to comprehension, and in fact even after Bontempelli had made peace with the play and readmitted it into his canon, he still found it "a big mess."[121] And yet, the play is strangely moving. It has a heart many of his other plays lack, and one can't help but think that the death of the author's own infant daughter had inspired both the story and a particular sympathy for the heartbroken Maria — in this, the play was a whole different kind of goodbye from the others Bontempelli so habitually enacted. The second scene seems a perfect realization of the magic realist quest "to cover with smiles" her despair. Her nutty determination to explain her rescue plan to the Deputy is as touching as it is amusing.

Maria's *candore* resides in numerous aspects of her personality and actions. She is utterly uninhibited by social codes, and in this is a perfectly Bontempellian anti-bourgeois. None of the troubles of the standard love triangle — the basis for much bourgeois theater of the day — bother her. She was abandoned by her lover, because he already has a family, but this isn't at issue. In fact, when she finds him with a new woman at the same hotel they had once visited together, she feels neither embarrassment nor jealousy but only seeks to save the two from future despair. Others' visions of the world are so antithetical to hers that there is no cause for disagreement. She simply doesn't understand reality in the same way — this we see when the heartbroken nuns are incapable of making her realize that her baby is not sleeping but dead. It's clear that Maria's been driven

---

121. Letter from Bontempelli to Nino Frank, Rome, February 26, [n.d. but 1924], Alvaro et al., *Lettere a "900,"* 74. Bontempelli wrote, for instance, that perhaps the innkeeper scene could be cut, but then it would just have to be replaced with something else.

Introduction

mad by her daughter's death. It is also true that the consequences of her miscomprehension are tragic, for while she is convinced that she will save the world by obstructing the moonlight, she will of course herself be responsible for its destruction as well as her own demise.[122] But Maria's madness — the focus of much criticism to date — has been overemphasized and interpreted as the weakness that brings her downfall. What's appealing, and curious and complex, about her credulity isn't the madness. Instead, it's the fearlessness and determination that it gives her: *candore* is the wellspring of her action and what grants her the strength to go on. She is, as her creator described the *candida*, "divinely imprudent," and this propels her to see her life as a mission, as an adventurous miracle that is hers to make.

Regina, on the other hand, seems to shrink away from such audacity. The nineteen-year-old protagonist of *Stormcloud* actually describes herself as prudent, but she would be better defined as grounded: *candore* doesn't spur her to extraordinary action, like her Bontempellian sisters, but makes her resolute in her attachment to the present. In the play's first episode, we learn that eight years before, a mysterious cloud — the *nembo* of the play's title — descended on the town and killed many of its children, including Regina's little sister. This experience taught the young survivor that the most important thing in life is "to play." For this reason she is reluctant to accept a marriage proposal from either of the two men, Marzio and Felice, who court her, because marriage seems entirely too serious a thing. So, she plays, literally, with the children in town, even while she lives with a sense of foreboding — and this with good reason, for soon the cloud returns, bringing death once more. Ever a child despite her years, she resembled Bontempelli, who one critic dubbed "the white-haired youngster with spring in his heart."[123] But soon Regina slumps to the ground, seemingly dead: proof positive for all that she was really still a child, or as Marzio put it, that she died of "too much innocence."

The play is enigmatic and not without its faults — even if a talented young dramatist–critic Cesare Vico Lodovici called it "the sunniest moment in the day" of its author's theatrical opus — but

---

122. Namer, *Massimo Bontempelli*, 169–71.
123. "Significato di Bontempelli," (n.p.).

Introduction

a striking example of what magic realism could be on the stage.[124] Dated to 1935, it follows upon *Bassano, padre geloso* (*Bassano, Jealous Father*, 1932), *Valòria* — neither of which met with much success — and *La fame* (*Hunger*, 1934) — which was barred from the stage in early 1935 on Mussolini's orders.[125] *La Fame* features the conflict between a megalomaniac dictator and a woman named Barbara, who returns to town after many years and, now wealthy, wishes to provide for all those who are hungry, as she once was. But when Barbara re-encounters Sira, the first woman who deprived her of food, she instead is seized by the thirst for revenge. She kills the woman and then stands there immobile on stage. After this traumatic event, her suffering prevents her not only from doing good, but from acting at all. (This story will sound familiar to anyone who has read Friedrich Dürrenmatt's play *Der Besuch der alten Dame* (*The Visit,* 1956); and indeed, Bontempelli attempted to sue the Swiss writer for plagiarism but, since ideas and plots are not protected by copyright as language is, inevitably lost the case.)[126] All of these plays mark a partial shift in theme for Bontempelli in the 1930s: if *Dea* and *Minnie* explore the individual, personal ramifications of social crises, these works investigate the communal, social consequences of individual human pathology.

This may already be less true for *Stormcloud,* where a nimbus, rather than an individual — be it jealous father, violent dictator or crazed avenger — is responsible for misery and destruction. In the world of this play, innocence itself is under attack, as highlighted in

---

124. Cesare Vico Lodovici, "Massimo Bontempelli nel teatro del 900," *Scenario* 4 (1941): 242.
125. As the archival paper trail is incomplete, no one has reconstructed the events behind the banning of *Hunger*. In his notes to the 1947 *Teatro* publication, Bontempelli acknowledged that Mussolini had been responsible for the veto, and Marinella Mascia Galateria has cited one surviving letter from censor Leopoldo Zurlo to Bontempelli that confirms this, in *Lettere a "900,"* 177n., as well as in her *Racconti allo specchio: Studi Bontempelliani* (Rome: Bulzoni, 2005), 70n., which also contains a brief but useful overview of Bontempelli's dramatic work. A search of newspaper articles further reveals that the show was pulled just days before its premier: whether this was the result of mere backlog in the approval process or an extraordinary intervention provoked by "public security" concerns, as the police monitored theatrical activity, isn't entirely clear, but Zurlo's letter does in some way suggest the former.
126. Alvise Memmo was kind to respond to my inquiries regarding Dürrenmatt.

Introduction

episode two when the funeral orator tells the crowd of parents not to mourn the loss of their innocent children, but to accept death as the highest form of life. And yet, this play too points fingers at individual behaviors and especially at personal egotism in the face of love and death. The living Regina wishes to be with the man who loves her most, and first seeks out Felice. But he rejects her, preferring to pass his days mourning a photo and an ideal of her, exalting his own abstract sentiments rather than living his life, in the present, with her. Marzio therefore gets his girl.

The fifth and final episode tenders a kind of reverse rewriting of *Watching the Moon*. The cloud has taken the children away, but the sky begins to brighten once again. Regina gazes above and imagines the children there, no longer mourning their death but seeing them as angels in a joyful place. From upstage, as if from out of that bright sky and out of death, happy, lively kids come a-running. They begin to play, inviting Regina and Marzio to join them. She encourages him, letting him know that the Marzio of episode one — the Marzio who asked for "order," told her to be serious and thought only of the future — won't do. He has "to learn to play." The girl who has come back to life teaches him, in other words, that *candore* is the way to happiness. Her way of seeing makes it so that, to recall the high priest from "Viaggio d'Europa" once again, "To die is to always be reborn."[127]

The Fairy Godmother in Bontempelli's 1942 *Cinderella* put down her wand in Prosperian fashion, and yet, as noted, in some ways she was just insisting upon what Bontempelli had always said — that magic wasn't anything but imagination or seeing with the "secret gaze." Cinderella learns her lesson well. Magic powers don't lie in the wand or the glass slipper, but in the eye of the beholder. Even if fairy magic gets her to the ball, from then on she determines her own path. It is her sense of truth and reality that eventually brings her happiness. Cinderella's is finally a story that ends well, and this is thanks to the *candore* evident not least in the fact that she can't even abide by the codes her fable lays out for her. She is, after all, a Cinderella who rejects Prince Charming.

There is a joyful simplicity about her, but this doesn't suggest an absolute naivety and shouldn't overshadow her determination. She is firm in standing up to the prince, insistent in pushing him

---

127. In *Opere Scelte*, 456.

Introduction

toward the kinder of her two stepsisters, Antonia, and resolute in her choice to be with Icarus. But the young girl's *candida* spirit is perhaps most insistently displayed in her trip to the ball. From the start, she breaks all the rules, first because she doesn't know what they are, and then because she has the courage to do so if she judges them unsatisfying. Bontempelli had said that the *candida* had trouble understanding the language of others, and this we see is one of Cinderella's greatest difficulties at the ball. Like Minnie before her, she is repeatedly forced to ask what a term or a rule means, or why it is important. Typically, she rebels against the rules of the world in which she finds herself and is simply turned off by its speech, even saying to the prince, who plays the gallant, "How difficultly you speak!"

That Cinderella's *candore* is the source of her strength becomes clear when it turns out that breaking the magic spell saves her, for this is what puts her — not just figuratively — on the path toward home. The seeming disaster begins, as always, when she nearly misses the stroke of midnight, this time because she doesn't understand the clue: when the grand mid quadrille is announced, she doesn't realize that the "mid" stands for midnight, and as she dances away, the chimes move inexorably toward the witching hour. She barely escapes, but when she does, finds herself on the road home, no longer the "Celestial Angel" she appeared to be at the palace, but a disheveled and clog-clomping girl again. In this guise she meets Icarus once more, and he sees beyond the surface to recognize her all the same. The prince, even if out searching for his angel, when he stumbles upon her sees only an idiot, and an ugly one at that.

Bontempelli composed music for *Cinderella*, as he had done for *Siepe a nordovest* and *Nostra Dea*, and the use of it — particularly through the two songs, "The Choruses of the Earth and Sky" — invites further reflection on the *candida* spirit.[128] Cinderella and Icarus share the ability to see beyond surface reality, but also to

---

128. Unlike with his other plays, Bontempelli didn't publish the music for *Cinderella*, but it is archived at the GRI 32. For an analysis of it, see Aurora Cogliandro, "Valenza della musica in 'Nostra Dea' e 'Cenerentola,'" in Donati, ed., *Massimo Bontempelli scrittore e intellettuale*, 269–92. On the play, see also Luigi Fontanella, "Sull'estrema produzione drammaturgica di Massimo Bontempelli: *Cenerentola* tra musical e fiaba teatrale," *L'illuminista* 5.13–15 (2005): 453–68.

hear beyond it. In act one, the fairy godmother and Cinderella listen to the Earth song: hearing it requires no magic, just listening hard. In act three, Cinderella sits with Icarus in the woods, and they look at the sky, listening to its chorus together. So doing, they understand the mysteries of the universe, and as the godmother had explained to Cinderella, this understanding, the *candida*'s elemental intelligence, was all that magic was: "The greatest magic is intelligence, from which goodness is born: that is the spell for being happy." There in the woods with Icarus — in what Bontempelli called the solitude of poetry — Cinderella's happiness is born.[129] The play's finale poetically suggests that Cinderella and Icarus will together persist in this solitude, a rejection of the prince's world of wealth, social rituals and even proscribed marriage. On the prince's command, a procession toward the palace to celebrate the nuptials begins. But Cinderella and Icarus grasp hands: they lag behind, and as the bugles sound, ever further off, they remain.

The couple's immobility recalls that of their creator: this is their moment of pause, the moment in which they square their own shoulders before starting down the new walk they've designed for themselves, in complete and total *candore*. It's not Bontempelli's first theatrical finale built upon such an instant. In 1925 he concluded *Nostra Dea* with a similar moment of stasis — a refuge in silent immobility, in reflection — before the creative burst of Novecento.[130] The instant of arrest was surely an important one for Bontempelli's characters because it was important for him, too. He had commented that Bragaglia was known the world over as a great barbarian, "because only a barbarian can be so *candido* as to still believe in the theater and dedicate his life to renewing it."[131] But

---

129. When Bontempelli prefaced an Italian poetry collection in 1943, he wrote that "Poetry is the resistance of the human spirit, which wants to return to the sky, against history, which wants to accommodate it on earth." It was here he wrote of the "solitude of poetry," as well. *Lirica italiana: Dal Cantico delle creature al Canto notturno d'un pastore errante dell'Asia* (Milan: Bompiani, 1943), xii.

130. On the moment of pause in *Nostra Dea*, see Patricia Gaborik, "La Donna Mobile: Massimo Bontempelli's *Nostra Dea* as Fascist Modernism," *Modern Drama* 50.2 (2007): 210–32. For a compelling discussion of dramatic finales in general and some of Bontempelli's plays in particular, including the symbolic and inconclusive "disappearance into the void" of Maria in *Watching the Moon*, see Beatrice Alfonzetti, *Drammaturgia della fine: Da Eschilo a Pasolini* (Rome: Bulzoni, 2008).

131. "Giusto giudizio su Bragaglia," 353.

Introduction

this could have just as easily been said about Bontempelli himself. If Bontempelli frequently became the protagonist of his own stories and the possessor of the "secret gaze," in the dramatic works his alter ego is most often that *candida* whose journey unfolds on stage. That *candore* is so intrinsic to Bontempelli is suggested by the fact that it appears so consistently in the dramas, from the beginning to the end of his career. His clamorous rejections — even of the theater he continued to write for — rose up to punch potholes in the Bontempellian terrain. But rather than seeing the author as the king of chameleons, we ought to imagine him as the Icarus who holds Cinderella's hand, as she — like the rest of Bontempelli's *candide* — runs gleefully across that land, hopping over the potholes as children do puddles after a rainstorm.

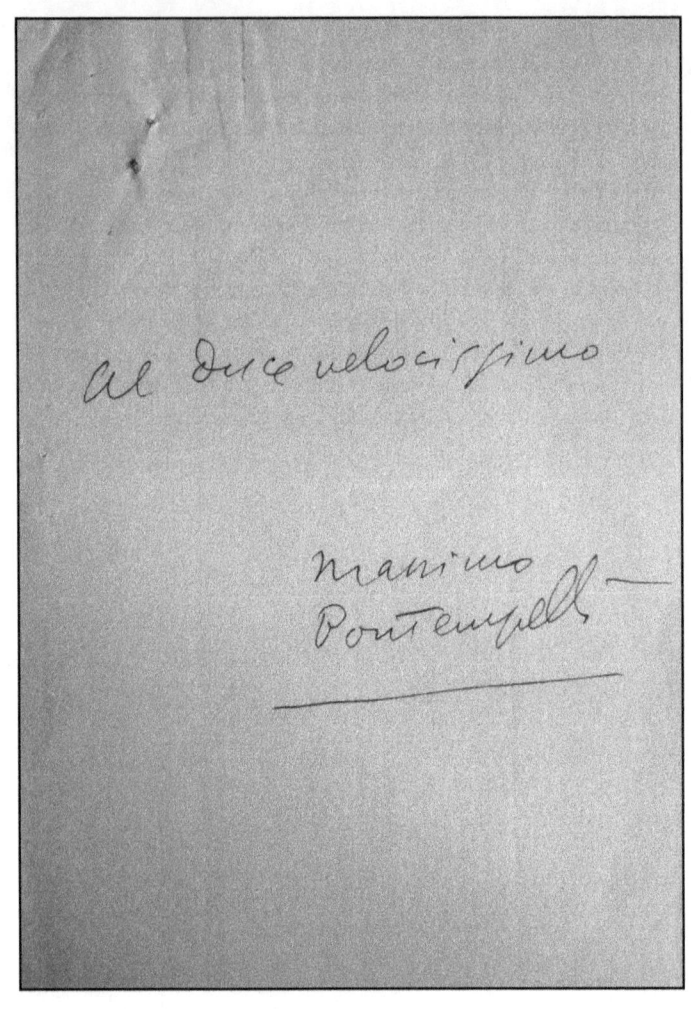

Bontempelli's dedication "to the super-fast duce."
Courtesy of Archivio Centrale dello Stato, Roma.

A Note on the Translations

Plays are meant to be played. When I decided to translate these texts, it was not simply so that an Anglophone audience could read them, but also because I believe they contain exciting performance possibilities. I have concentrated on making the plays producible for a contemporary English-speaking audience, but this doesn't suggest any "infidelity" on my part, nor any changing or eliminating of unfamiliar references (where necessary, I've included footnotes). To the contemporary ear, some of Bontempelli's language sounds a bit antiquated or hyper-literary — a problem not uncommon for Italian drama of the era — while on the other hand, traces of attempts to write plausible dialogue abound (a look at his punctuation, where many commas separate very short phrases, for instance, indicate that he was writing with oral delivery in mind, even without necessarily exactly replicating natural speech). I've attempted to respect the spirit and environment of the plays while keeping in mind the actors who will speak his words. As a result, the translations at times read more "smoothly" than the originals do — from a contemporary perspective, anyway — and in this demonstrate an attention to "speakability" analogous to Bontempelli's. His sense of theatricality was unparalleled, his characters are bewitching; privileging playability seems to me the best "fidelity" I can offer him and the best chance I can give the plays for life not only on page but also on stage.

Bontempelli was not first and foremost a playwright. At times, it seems that the novelist in him prevailed, so that stage directions frequently describe what a reader must imagine — rather than, say, what a designer must create for an audience to see — or explain what has happened in the meantime — instead of what a character now does to move the action forward. Where it was possible without disrupting the rhythm, and where it seemed most important, I took the liberty of transforming these narrative descriptions into tried and true stage directions: instructions for the actors and creative team, which for the reader function as "real-time" unfolding of the action. In *Stormcloud* more than in others, Bontempelli tended to overwrite, giving indications, such as "They begin to protest," that are made superfluous by the dialogue. Such directions have been largely eliminated.

A Note on the Translations

One aspect of the language that heightens the plays' unreality — or magic realist qualities — is the incongruence between the rather "high" language and the *"candide"* characters who speak it, like *Stormcloud*'s Regina (on the *candida*, see the introduction). Another particular challenge is posed by the philosophical riffs of characters like the Innkeeper (in *Moon*) and Marzio (in *Stormcloud*): in this latter, his discourse sits somewhat uncomfortably within the contained, rather rapid rhythm the play otherwise employs. As noted in the introduction, Bontempelli recognized that such moments in *Moon* were problematic and perhaps the only hope was to just eliminate them; here they of course remain.

A word must be said about the Italian dialects and foreign languages in *Watching the Moon*. Two characters speak regional dialects: the Emigrant from the Abruzzo (a rural, mountainous region in south-central Italy important for the rearing of livestock) and the Bawd, who speaks with the dialect of Milan, the northern city that was a capital of industry then as it is now. There is no true equivalent for such differences in American English — Italian dialects can be so different from region to region that they are mutually unintelligible. An Italian audience would have perceived a stark difference in these characters' speech, and Bontempelli was obviously invested in rendering that contrast. The reader will see a much less formal tone in the scenes where the Emigrant and the Bawd appear; this is due to the "popular" nature of dialect as well as to the fact that, whereas throughout most of the play the characters address one another with the formal third-person "Lei" or the still more formal and somewhat archaic "Voi," the familiar "tu" dominates the interactions in these scenes. (Maria continues to use the polite form "lei" even with those who address her with the "tu" in the brothel scene.) In performance, to further increase the contrast in register for the characters who speak dialect, a director could consider using strong accents and/or alterations of key words in the lines. Such choices depend so heavily on the local parlance where the play is to be performed that it seems to me more useful to signal the problem and invite directors to provide fitting solutions. Additionally, there is a French courtesan in the cast of characters. Here I have kept the French in the English text; though many of Bontempelli's audience members — unlike a contemporary Anglophone public — would have known the language, the rupture produced by the sudden imposition of a

A Note on the Translations

foreign idiom is too important to renounce here. Translations are included in the footnotes.

Finally, the reader will note a curiosity in Bontempelli's labeling. *Watching the Moon* is subtitled "A Play," — in Italian, the word is "Rappresentazione." In a theatrical context the word is best understood as "performance," in current usage common for referring to a particular staging, as on a given evening. In Italian, medieval mystery plays were called "rappresentazioni sacre," and the resonances with aspects of *Watching the Moon,* in particular the episodic nature it shares with contemporary expressionist drama as well as the mystery play, suggest to me that the equivalent "Play" is the best choice. In that same vein, Bontempelli's "Quadro" here becomes "Episode." "Quadro" was not uncommon in plays of the epoch, and the term could simply be translated as "scene." However, there seems to be something especially significant for Bontempelli in this choice: "quadro" is also the word used for a painting, indicating a somewhat "fixed" enactment that has ties to the archetypes we find in mystery plays and expressionist drama alike. Given that Bontempelli uses "quadro" within a "rappresentazione," the sense of a fixed image, a sort of tableau of life, emerges particularly clearly. What's more, the playwright only used "quadro" in the three plays of this volume, which tend toward the episodic rather than the continuous (in which case, he uses the standard act ("atto") structure. In fact "quadro" is only used with the two plays that Bontempelli calls "Rappresentazioni" *(Watching the Moon* and *Stormcloud)* and the one subtitled "Spectacle" or "Show," *Cinderella.* In that play, the "quadri" appear within the acts, but they function in a similarly episodic way. The strongest, most curious choice Bontempelli puts forward, however, is that of "Persone" (People, or persons) rather than the traditional "Personaggio" (Character). This is, quite honestly, a choice difficult to square with the more distant view encouraged by "Rappresentazione" and "Quadro." In all of his plays but one *(L'Innocenza di Camilla),* Bontempelli defaulted to "People" (in *Camilla,* he uses "Characters").

Particulars, including those that concern the plays' and characters' names, I've addressed in the notes to the individual texts.

Further Reading

Bontempelli in Translation

Fiction

Bontempelli, Massimo. *The Chess Set in the Mirror.* Translated by Estelle Gilson. Philadelphia: Paul Dry Books, 2007.

—.*The Faithful Lover.* Translated by Estelle Gilson. Austin, TX: Host Publications, 2007.

—. *Separations: Two Novels of Mothers and Children.* Translated by Estelle Gilson. Kingston, NY: McPherson & Co, 2000.

Drama

Bontempelli, Massimo. *Dea by Dea.* Translated by Anthony Oldcorn in Jane House and Antonio Attisani, *Twentieth-Century Italian Drama: An Anthology, the First Fifty Years.* New York: Columbia University Press, 1995.

—. *The Divine Miss D* and *Genuine Minnie* in Jack D. Street and Rod Umlas. *The Italian Theater of the Grotesque: A New Theater for the Twentieth Century. An Anthology,* Lewiston, NY: Edwin Mellen, 2003.

Secondary Literature

There is currently no monograph available on Bontempelli in English. In addition to the works appearing in the notes to my introduction, I include here a few other English-language works of interest:

Campbell, Timothy C. "'Infinite Remoteness': Marinetti, Bontempelli, and the Emergence of Modern Visual Culture." *MLN* 120 (2005): 111–36.

Gaborik, Patricia. "La Donna Mobile: Massimo Bontempelli's *Nostra Dea* as Fascist Modernism." *Modern Drama* 50.2 (2007): 210–32.

Segel, Harold B. 'From Puppets to Artificial Men: The Darkening Vision of Massimo Bontempelli,' section of chapter nine, "Italian Futurism, Teatro Grottesco, and the World of Artificial Man." In *Pinocchio's Progeny: Puppets, Marionettes, Automatons, and Robots in Modernist and Avant-Garde Drama.* Baltimore; Johns Hopkins University Press, 1995.

Luca Somigli. "Modernism and the Quest for the Real: On Massimo Bontempelli's *Minnie la candida*." In *Italian Modernism: Italian Culture between Decadentism and Avant-Garde,* edited by Mario Moroni and Luca Somigli. Toronto: University of Toronto Press, 2004, 309–50.

ANNO II - N. 7   Conto Corrente colla Posta   10 Aprile 1920

COMOEDIA

FASCICOLO PERIODICO DI COMMEDIE E DI VITA TEATRALE

Questo numero contiene:

MASSIMO BONTEMPELLI

LA GUARDIA ALLA LUNA

Commedia in sette quadri rappresentata per la prima volta a Milano al Teatro Olympia il 15 Marzo 1920 dalla Compagnia di Virgilio Talli

M. Bontempelli CENNO BIOGRAFICO
Maria Valsecchi MEDAGLIONE
Rassegna Teatrale DI GINO ROCCA

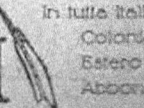

CASA EDITRICE ITALIA
— Milano —
Corso VIII. Emanuele, 8
— Telefoni 40-06 — 40-12 —

In tutta Italia, prezzo L. 1.50
Colonie . . . . . » 1.50
Estero . . . . . » 2.—
Abbon. a 12 num. » 15.—
     »   24   »   » 30.—

Direttore Amministrativo: EUGENIO GANDOLFI

Watching the Moon

A Play

Massimo Bontempelli

A Note on the Text

I've translated *La guardia alla luna* from the 1947 volume, *Teatro I* (Milan: Mondadori), which contains some slight differences from the version first published in *Primo Spettacolo* by Mondadori in 1927, maintaining the revisions already present in the 1936 volume published by Edizioni di Novissima.

Written in 1916, *Watching the Moon* premiered in Milan in 1920 with what Bontempelli considered a superb performance by Maria Melato, but nonetheless finished, in the author's words, under "a hurricane of boos" — and was shut down after that opening. The reviewer for *Il Primato* observed that the author of such a play must have had "a strange mix of genius and blindness," but the show would be remembered as one of the legendary disasters in Italian theater for years to come. Bontempelli's vengeance came nearly a decade later, in 1929, when a tiny Roman avant-garde house called *Teatro del 2000*, which also exhumed Marinetti's *Re Baldoria*, but unsuccessfully, reprised the play. If critics still had their doubts, many acknowledged that the play had a "humanity" particularly notable for such a seemingly cold and ironic writer, and the popular audience was so enthusiastically moved to call performers and author for twenty bows. The critic for *Il Resto del Carlino* quipped, "in any case, these ten years were useful even for the theater," which had found an audience to applaud a work that had failed so miserably on its first go-round. The play was also produced in South America in 1929, in Romania in the late 1930s and 40s — Bontempelli traveled frequently to Eastern Europe and enjoyed success there — and at a small theater in Pavia (Italy), by director and protagonist Anna Maria Meschini, in 1943.

P.G.

Watching the Moon

Characters

MARIA

LOTS OF MEN AND WOMEN

Episode One

Maria's room. Downstage right, nearly in the wings, a cradle covered with a white veil; flowers scattered about the veil and at the head and foot of the cradle. A tall candle on each side. An exit upstage toward the left. A window upstage right.

A NUN *stands in the threshold of the upstage exit, leaning against the door frame; she is silent. A* WOMAN *stands center stage, between the door and the cradle. A* SECOND WOMAN *sits in a corner, her head bowed.* MARIA *sits next to the cradle with her arm draped across it. She turns to the* WOMAN.

MARIA She's sleeping now. There's no need to speak softly anymore.

WOMAN No, there's no need…

MARIA When she's fallen asleep she doesn't hear anything anymore. Even when he still came — he made lots of noise with his shoes — she went on sleeping. She wasn't even a year old. Now, yes. Fifteen months. She's walking. You didn't see her walk. You only have to hold her for a minute, because she is still a little afraid to let go. But then, she's off — she crosses the whole room: all the way to there. You'll see her in a few days, when we can sit her up and dress her. Do you promise you'll come right away to see her walk?

WOMAN …Yes, yes.

MARIA But why are you still crying? She's well now, don't you know? There's no more danger of anything. Don't you think?

WOMAN I know. I know there's no more danger.

MARIA See? When I take one of her arms like this, she calms down, and she falls asleep. This means that she's well. These past few days, you remember? She didn't recognize me, and nothing would keep her quiet. Now look. She doesn't even move. She's cured, cured — completely. She sleeps so soundly!

WOMAN Alright, then. Come into the other room. Come rest a bit.

NUN *(whispers)* Everything is ready downstairs.

MARIA What did she say?

WOMAN She said everything is ready in there, to eat. Come and get something. Do you know it's been three days since you've eaten?

MARIA Just a minute. I'll wait a little to lift my arm, so I don't wake her. Back then, too, he would often come and call me — he was in a hurry for me to come to bed — and if I lifted my arm from here too soon, she woke up right away. When he no longer came, sometimes I fell asleep here, like this. When I woke up I was so cold.

NUN *(whispers)* We have to go…

WOMAN Come.

MARIA Yes, yes. Where?

WOMAN In there. To get something —

MARIA What is there to get?

WOMAN Something to eat.

MARIA Not on your life!

NUN *(with frightened impatience)* It's late.

MARIA For what?

WOMAN Yes, it's late. Look, *(pointing out the window, where the moon now lights the entire sky)* the moon is already high. Then you have to go to sleep, too. You need it badly. Ten nights!

MARIA *(bewildered)* Am I sleepy?

WOMAN Blessed virgin!

The NUN *makes the sign of the cross. Pause. The* WOMAN *approaches* MARIA *and, from behind, gently lifts her to her feet.* MARIA *lets her. She keeps her arm outstretched over the cradle momentarily, then she turns to the* WOMAN, *as if she is waking up.*

MARIA It's true. I'm sorry.

The NUN *comes to* MARIA*'s other side. They take a few steps toward the exit.*

MARIA *(stopping)* Where are we going?

Watching the Moon

NUN   Come, come.

MARIA   I would prefer to stay here. If she wakes up?

NUN   I'll come right back.

WOMAN   There you go. You go in there. Have a little something to eat, and then take a nap. The sister and I will stay here until you return.

They begin to move her again.

MARIA   *(lets herself be led, murmuring)* It's not the same. It's not the same.

They pass by the window. Outside the moon lights up the sky.

MARIA   Won't there be a draft?

NUN   No, no.

MARIA   Won't there soon be too much light? All that moon!

WOMAN   Stay calm. Come.

MARIA   But to sleep I'm coming back here.

NUN   Yes, yes.

At the door, MARIA *stops, turns toward the cradle and gently imitates her own manner of keeping her arm above the cradle.*

MARIA   *(toward the cradle, with a soft whisper)* I'll be right back.

They exit. The SECOND WOMAN *gets up and looks expectantly at the door. After a moment the* NUN *returns.*

NUN   *(in a trembling whisper)* On with it.

The NUN *goes to the cradle, takes up the bundled little body and follows the* SECOND WOMAN *out the door. They go quickly, silently. The moonlight enters through the window and shines above the cradle. Subdued murmurs of prayer come from the street. They grow distant and suddenly stop. After a short pause,* MARIA *reappears in the doorway, held back by the* WOMAN.

MARIA   What was that?

WOMAN   Nothing, I tell you. Come.

MARIA   I thought I heard something... *(begins to cross to the cradle)*

WOMAN   *(holding her back)* Don't wake her.

Massimo Bontempelli

MARIA   I can't see very well.... Look, the moon is almost to the cradle. We have to close the window.

WOMAN   Yes, yes. Come back. I'll do it.

MARIA   Just a minute. *(She halts, listening with an ear extended toward the cradle.)* I think she's waking up!

MARIA *breaks free and runs on tip-toes to the cradle. She bows down over it. The* WOMAN *has followed her but no longer even tries to pull her away.*

WOMAN   Mother Mary, help me!

MARIA   Little one.... Little...! *(She gropes about the blankets, feverishly)* Where is she? Where is she? *(with a piercing shriek)* Ah! She's not here! Help! *(She searches the cradle furiously, knocking it over.)* They've taken her away! Run, run! Call someone! *(Running across the room)* Help! *(She falls to the ground.)*

The WOMAN *runs out.*

MARIA   *(unable to stand, groping)* Who took her from me? Who took her away from me? I want her, I want her!... *(wheezing, her gaze fixed on the cradle, which is now completely bathed in moonlight, she screams again, even louder)* Ah!... *(She rises and with a leap is at the cradle.)* It was her. It was the moon. She took her from me. She took her away. *(She turns to the light, which illuminates everything, and with arms outstretched, her whole body trembling, she drags herself toward the window.)* Damn you — I see you — I saw you — give her back to me.... Little one, little one, don't go away. Come, come back to your mama.... Ah, she can't hear. Shameless thief, give her back. I'll kill you, you thief! You murderer!

MARIA *throws herself on the windowsill, lifting her head and raising her arms as if she wants to climb toward the sky. The* WOMAN *and the* NUN *run in and pull* MARIA *away from the window. On contact,* MARIA *screams, frees herself from them and falls to the ground, gasping, raising her fist toward the window.*

NUN   Mother Mary! Help me, hold her tight!

The NUN *and the* WOMAN *prepare to lift* MARIA *as the scene goes black, then changes.*

Watching the Moon

Episode Two

The deputy's study.

The DEPUTY *is seated at his desk. A knock on the door.*

DEPUTY   Come in.

MAN   *(entering)* Sir.

DEPUTY   Yes.

MAN   Um….

DEPUTY   What do you want? Speak up. I'm in a hurry.

MAN   I wanted to report…that I am certain…yes, I have the proof…that my wife betrays me —

DEPUTY   Office B, second door on the left *(with a wave).*

MAN   Ah…. Thank you.

The MAN *exits. A* BAILIFF *enters.*

DEPUTY   Are there others?

BAILIFF   A young woman.

DEPUTY   Let her in.

The BAILIFF *exits.* MARIA *enters.*

DEPUTY   How may I help you?

MARIA   *(She is very serious, sure, precise.)* Sir, I have come to report a grave matter, with which I need your help.

DEPUTY   Go on, miss.

MARIA   I have a child. A daughter.

DEPUTY   How old?

MARIA   Fifteen months.

DEPUTY   I'll have to take notes, and I'll need your name as well. But meanwhile, go on, ma'am.

MARIA   This child got lost.

DEPUTY   Lost! A child of fifteen months!

MARIA   Listen. She was in the cradle. She had been sick ten days. Then she was better, and she slept. I went in the other room for a moment. I come back, she wasn't there anymore.

DEPUTY But then someone kidnapped her.

MARIA Exactly.

DEPUTY At what time did this happen?

MARIA Around eight in the evening.

DEPUTY Last night?

MARIA No. Nine days ago.

DEPUTY And you're just reporting it now?

MARIA Because I know exactly where she is and who took her. I discovered it right away.

DEPUTY Then please explain.

MARIA You must be patient because the matter is a bit complicated. You need to know that the baby's father was my friend.

DEPUTY I see.

MARIA And when the baby was ten months old, he no longer came. You know, for his reasons…because of his family…it doesn't matter. So I was left alone with the baby. And now you must be patient, and we'll back up.

DEPUTY If instead we moved forward, and you told me who kidnapped —

MARIA No, excuse me, you couldn't understand it all. You need to know that the first time my friend and I said we loved each other, it was evening, in the country, on a terrace. And the moon was there…

DEPUTY So?

MARIA The entire valley was lit by the moon, all the grass, all the plants. And there were lots and lots of fireflies, all moon drops, all throughout the air.

DEPUTY *(resigned)* Alright.

MARIA You cannot understand yet. His voice was like I had never heard before. I told him that. And he said, "It's the voice of the moon, who wants you to be mine." In fact, it did seem to me like the moon was speaking. I remember that I didn't look at her, up there in the sky, because I was ashamed, but I felt her. I felt her light, her voice. She was no longer cold, as usual. She was warm and she wrapped up the whole world, and she hugged me, really just like a voice. She entered my soul. And I didn't know anymore if it was the moon who was speaking to me, or if it was him hugging me with light. *(She is about to break down.)*

DEPUTY   But ma'am… miss…

MARIA   So, even after that, he always said that he had placed our love under the moon's protection. It was true.

DEPUTY   I beg you…

MARIA   *(getting up, with a restrained quivering)* It was true! When he left me, I felt that the moon had turned cold toward me, even mean, yes, mean, I tell you. And I didn't know why. What had I done to her? I believed her. I surrendered to her…. And yet I felt that she bore me ill will. I felt suspicious, and I didn't understand why and it seemed to me that I was being unjust. Ah…

DEPUTY   Ma'am, I beg you to calm down…and to come to the point.

MARIA   I'm sorry. You still cannot understand. It took me all this time to understand — all these days since she took my little one away from me. She was cured, she was sleeping well, calm. It seemed like she wasn't even breathing. All it took…. I just went out for a minute…. I thought I heard something, I don't know, a noise or a presentiment. I go back to the cradle — she wasn't there, do you understand? All the flowers were there, strewn about the cradle, but not her. And the light of the moon was still all over the cradle — you understand? — laughing. She had taken her away, with the veil they wrapped her in. I still saw her, up above, far away, my little one, going up on the light, and I called to her, but she couldn't answer; she couldn't turn back. She vanished. She's there, sir. She's up there, and I know that I might never be able to have her back ever again. *(She cries.)*

DEPUTY   Dear lady, calm down…. Yes, I understand. Everything you have told me is…quite exact, logical. It was inevitable. What can you do? These are great misfortunes…that befall us. Now you need to calm down. There is nothing to be done…. But, that's just it, you have discovered all on your own who abducted your poor baby. Consequently I don't see…how I can be of help to you.

Massimo Bontempelli

MARIA *(regaining her composure, serious)* Well, as soon as I discovered the crime, I set myself to thinking. I locked myself in, all alone. And it's nine days that I've been thinking, thinking hard, fixated, about this. And I get it! Listen. I realized that the moonlight that stole my baby was the very same light — the very same! — as that night that I gave myself to my friend. The same, but it spoke no more. It was mean. She stopped pretending. She didn't need to trick me anymore, you see?[1] And so, rethinking so hard of all that had happened in my life, between me and the moon, from that first night until this last, I discovered something, something terrible. The moon comes over the world, over the whole world, to bring lovers together so that they will love each other — so babies are born — and then, listen, and then, those girls who the lovers abandon and they end up alone when the babies are still little, she takes them away from them. She takes them up, in the sky. She needs babies, because her light is made of the babies she steals. That's why she brings so many lovers together and then keeps watch over the whole world at night, intent on knowing where the girls who are left alone in the world with their children are. *(pause)* I see that you are convinced. Now listen. For me — as for me — it's over. I know that I'll probably never have… my baby…here again. And I don't think that I can go and join her there. But for what is left of my life, a great mission has appeared to me. Do you know what it is? To prevent the moon from keeping on with this wickedness. The moonlight mustn't arrive on earth. Then she won't be able to steal babies anymore, and little by little she will have no more light, and she will die, and the world will be free.

Pause.

---

1. Maria, referring to the moonlight, uses the feminine pronoun. However, in the original text what is here translated as "moonlight" is not "luce," a feminine term, but "lume," a masculine term. Even though the semantic difference is minimal in this context, the gender difference becomes crucial. By referring to "moonlight" as "lume" and therefore a masculine term and force, Maria must use masculine pronouns while referring to the injustice done to her, though she then quickly begins to speak again of the female moon, "la luna." Here, in reference to the light, I have chosen the neutral pronoun "it," but in references to the moon itself, I have opted to keep the gendered "she": the personification "she" heightens the drama and is in keeping with a long literary tradition in which the moon is figured as a feminine. It is particularly apt given the play's engagement with the futurist's battle against the sentimental moon.

DEPUTY It's true, yes.

MARIA You've already seen what we must do.

DEPUTY Actually...

MARIA *(whispering, mysteriously)* We must find where the point is, the exact point, where the moonlight enters the earth.

DEPUTY Ah...

MARIA And close it. You understand? Am I explaining myself? Close it off, where it enters. Where it passes through. I feel up to doing this. I must do this, to free the world. I will close it, maybe with my own self. But first we must find it.

DEPUTY I don't see...

MARIA I've already thought about how to do the research. But first I thought it my duty to tell you about it, first of all because if you had heard talk of the baby's abduction...you would have accused some innocent while I had already found —

DEPUTY Exactly. Exactly. You did the right thing.

MARIA And then also because, for my venture, I was thinking: wouldn't it be useful if...you know, I could try, lead, but all by myself...

DEPUTY No, no. I believe I am giving you good counsel when I urge you to do it yourself. You who have found, so clearly, the key to the problem, you will be able to carry it through. And, in fact, I would say that it is the sort of thing that should remain top secret until it is done, because...because...

MARIA Yes, yes, I understand. One never knows.... There could be some accomplices....

DEPUTY Yes, that's it, exactly. Say nothing to no one. Do it yourself. I am very moved by your misfortune, ma'am, and I wish you all the best. *(gets up)* Believe me that if it seemed useful —

MARIA I perfectly understand. I am happy in any case to have confided in you and to have your encouragement. Be certain that I won't speak to a living soul. And *(resolute, but with a low, mysterious voice)* I will succeed.

DEPUTY I am sure of it.

MARIA Thank you. Thank you from the bottom of my heart.

MARIA *leaves accompanied by the* DEPUTY, *who bows to her and closes the door. Left alone, the* DEPUTY *sits again in his chair. He remains a minute, melancholy and pensive, shaking his head. A knock on the door.*

DEPUTY Come in.

The scene goes black, then changes.

Watching the Moon

Episode Three

The deck of a transatlantic oceanliner.

Two Sailors *seated downstage right. A song to the tune of "Algerian Xebec"*[2] *is heard, though the words cannot be distinguished. When the song ends, they speak.*

The One   It's lovely. It's an old, old song from the Genovese galleys. Our emigrants adopted it.

The Other   It's very sad. Do you want to go sit up there? *(indicates a bench above, on the middle deck, against the rail)*

The One   No. The lady will come soon. For fifteen days that's been her spot. Everyone respects it.

The Other   And no one has ever talked to her.

The One   I recognized her. I saw her a year ago, on the Zaghouan Mountain, in Tunisia.

The Other   There she is.

Maria *enters, goes to sit up top and sits staring at the sea.*

The Other   And then?

The One   That's all I know.

Enter an Adolescent Boy, *who sits at a little distance from* Maria, *below, and contemplates her in silence.*

The Other   All this sea overwhelms me. Tomorrow we'll hit land. Do you want to go below?

The One   Let's go below.

The Two Sailors *exit. Two chimes of the bell, from inside, like maritime signals. Enter* Two Other Sailors, *speaking as they pass.*

The First   She's already there.

The Second   I saw her two years ago, in a town at the foot of the Caucasus.

The First   Yesterday that boy talked to her.

The Second   And what about her?

---

2.   The Algerian xebec was a well-known type of ship, and a favorite of pirates cruising the Italian coast. The sight of it, therefore, often warned of an imminent attack.

Massimo Bontempelli

THE FIRST Nothing.

The TWO OTHER SAILORS *exit in the other direction. Two trumpet signals from inside.*

BOY *(to* MARIA, *without moving from his place, with contained passion)* May I speak to you?

MARIA No.

BOY Why don't you ever want to answer me?

MARIA You can't know.

BOY But it's the last night. Tomorrow I won't see you any more. Listen to me.

MARIA I can't. It's not because of you. I have a duty ahead of me that's…too great.

BOY Any minute now the moon will rise.… Oh, no. Wait.

MARIA No.

MARIA *gets up.*

BOY *(exasperated)* Listen. On my life, I swear to you that if you don't stay and listen to me, I'll kill myself. Now.

MARIA Farewell.

BOY You don't believe my oath? You don't think it's true that I'll kill myself?

MARIA *(For the first time, she looks momentarily into his eyes.)* I believe your oath.

BOY *(anxious)* And so?

MARIA There's something…greater.

MARIA *goes. The* ADOLESCENT BOY *remains alone, stupefied, motionless. He goes to sit where* MARIA *had been and stares out at the waves. After a while an* EMIGRANT WOMAN *from the Abruzzo enters and approaches him.*

EMIGRANT WOMAN What're you doing, mister? Watching the water? Don't watch the water. It's nasty, even when it's calm. Look at beautiful young ladies, now that you're young and rich, mister. Who knows what'll become of us tomorrow! No one knows.… What's wrong, handsome? What do you want to do?

Watching the Moon

Cast a spell on the ocean to resuscitate all the Christians, kind souls! All the Christians that the earth has stolen?!

BOY   No.

EMIGRANT WOMAN   What's wrong, handsome?

BOY   I have an oath to keep.

EMIGRANT WOMAN   If you made an oath, keep it, mister, because the oath of a Christian is God's will! Farewell, mister.

BOY   Good night.

The scene goes black, then changes.

Massimo Bontempelli

Episode Four

The crossroads in a rough quarter of a crowded city: a sort of narrow, irregular little square. Upstage the scene opens onto an alley. To the left a tavern. Upstage to the right, the façade of a brothel with all the windows illuminated. The light passes through the slats of the shutters, all closed, of the second-floor windows. On the first floor all the shutters are open, but the windows are veiled with white curtains. A few purplish lights shimmer at the end of the alley, a pink lantern at the tavern. The stage is empty. Sounds of a lullaby, sung by two female voices, come from the brothel. Then a soft hissing. The song stops abruptly, and five or six shadows pass indistinctly, one after the other, behind the illuminated curtains.

MARIA, *looking a bit frightened, enters from the alley and stops at the corner by the tavern, peering in the half-light. Meanwhile the lullaby begins again, softer.*

MARIA   This should be it. *(She tries to read the name of the alley.)* You can't see. *(She takes a box of matches from her pocket, tries to light one and breaks it, but then manages to light the next. She raises it in an effort to see.)* You can't see. *(She looks around and extends her ear toward the brothel, straining to hear.)* If I went and knocked there?

MARIA *is unsure. The lullaby stops. The* INNKEEPER *comes out from the tavern.*

INNKEEPER   What's all this signaling with matches?

MARIA   Excuse me. Can you tell me if this is Moon Alley?

INNKEEPER   Jupiter punish me if I haven't waited for something like this. I ask, you ask. In the schools they teach the verb "to love." They should teach the verb "to ask."[3]

MARIA   What?

INNKEEPER   I, you. Two human beings have suddenly met, and two questions have collided in the world. Every man — and I mean also every woman — is a question that travels the world in search of another question.

MARIA   Excuse me, I don't understand. I asked you, please, if this is Moon Alley. They told me it's in this town, around these parts.

---

3.   In English, the musicality of this line is lost. In Italian, "to love" is "amare," while "to ask" is "domandare."

Watching the Moon

INNKEEPER And I asked you something else. A jurist would dispute here about pre-judgments, to establish the right of precedence between these two questions. He would discuss it with the court until we go to our graves. Then my descendants would respond to your descendants, they would reveal the name of this spot of the universe. But I am not a jurist. I am therefore a man. And you, who are you? You too are a man, but a woman. That is, you are a question-female, who goes searching for, probably, one or more question-males. So I ask myself the question and give myself the answer to all the problems that present themselves to my very limited life.

MARIA Are you a philosopher?

INNKEEPER Jupiter savior! In thirty years of dwelling in this corner of the atom, everyone has taken me for an innkeeper. You are the first passer-by in these turbid places who realizes that I am the sediment of a philosopher, who understands this animal species. When I was still a man, and I was living far away from here, everyone mistook me for a philosopher, and no one had realized that the base of my destiny was to be an innkeeper.[4]

MARIA You didn't answer me.

INNKEEPER The best practice is to only ask the questions we can answer by ourselves. I do this with my regular customers. When one asks, "Innkeeper, do you have good wine?" I don't answer with words, I bring him the wine. And the customer later answers his own question, either by saying, "This innkeeper

---

4. The Innkeeper's philosophizing recalls Ancient Greek theories of metempsychosis, or transmigration of the soul from one being to another, prevalent, for example, also in Joyce's *Ulysses*. Bontempelli seems to be using an interesting double-entendre: in calling himself the sediment of a philosopher ("un fondo di filosofo") and referring to the "base of his destiny" ("il fondo del mio destino"), the Innkeeper uses language perfectly suited to an Innkeeper-philosopher: the "base" (or "fondo") is the bottom of a wine bottle, where the sediment (again "fondo") settles. Read this way, the line is a bitter observation on his sense of his own life, though it should be noted that Bontempelli did not use the term "feccia," which would lend itself to a translation like "dregs" — a far more negative term. As noted in the introduction, Bontempelli always had problems with this play, and this scene he considered particularly problematic, observing that, however, if it were cut, it would just need to be replaced with something else.

has excellent wine," or instead by swearing, "This innkeeper is a perfect poisoner."

MARIA   I really need to know if this is Moon Alley.

INNKEEPER   I really need to know where two people are: my master and my man. I call myself and say: servant, run inside to see what's happening in the cantina, or I'll give you the boot. And immediately I respond to myself: I'm coming, right away! If you enter, you will see that my wine is good, without you asking me about it.

MARIA   *(declining)* Thank you.

INNKEEPER   I see approaching from the base of that intestine a question-male,[5] who might fit you quite well, either by knife, or with some other, less bloody means.[6]

INNKEEPER *re-enters the tavern.* MARIA, *still a little frightened, draws close to the wall. A* PASSER-BY *comes from the end of the alley. Seeing* MARIA, *he crosses to the right to avoid her.*

MARIA   *(timidly)* Excuse me.... *(The* PASSER-BY *doesn't turn.)* Listen....

PASSER-BY   No, no. *(He crosses the stage diagonally toward the left.)*

MARIA   Sir....

The PASSER-BY *disappears upstage to the left.* MARIA *finds herself in the middle of the scene. The* BAWD *enters from the door of the brothel, having heard* MARIA *call out.*

BAWD   What'cha doing here?

MARIA   Excuse me, would you know how to point me —

BAWD   Go on, get lost. We got more than enough women around here. There's gotta be some other place you can go. *(She crosses to the tavern, calling to the* INNKEEPER.*)* You, sir. Two bottles of Marsala, right away. *(She enters the tavern.)*

---

5. Bontempelli invents a term, "un'interrogazione-maschio," perfectly in tune with the Innkeeper's philosophy of life as he has been describing it.
6. Here we have a case of bawdy humor: the Innkeeper suggests that the question-male will fit (into) Maria rather nicely and can do so either at knife-point or by persuading her in some more genteel fashion.

Watching the Moon

MARIA   Yet at this hour the moon must have risen.... If it's not here? *(with a resolute gesture)* Oh, it's getting really late!

MARIA *crosses to the brothel and knocks on the door. A* COURTESAN *appears in a window on the first floor. The door opens, the* DOORKEEPER, *with quite an ugly mug, peeks out. Her voice is raucous.*

DOORKEEPER   We're full. Come back in a half hour.

COURTESAN   Oh, c'est une femme, qu'est-ce que tu nous veux, salope? Maîtresse, venez voir.[7]

MADAM[8]   *(appears)* What do you want? Get going. Out of here. Snap to it.

MARIA *retreats, frightened. Some* COURTESANS *appear in the windows. The* MADAM *exits, shouting.*

MADAM   Inside, inside!

The COURTESANS *vanish. The* BAWD *enters from the tavern with two bottles.*

BAWD   What? You're still here? Get lost, stupid!

COURTESAN   *(reappears)* Mais il faudrait téléphoner aux gendarmes![9]

BAWD   No, no, forget it. (*to* MARIA) Go on now. The House of the Moon isn't a place for you to hang around.

MARIA   *(lets out a yelp)* The house of the Moon? But which one is the Moon's house?

MADAM   *(appearing, to the* BAWD) What are you doing down there? Bring it up, right away! (*to* MARIA) You still here? Ah, you just wait. Now we'll call for real. *(She goes back in.)*

BAWD   I'm coming, I'm coming. *(She whispers quickly to* MARIA.) And you run off now! Go on! *(She hurriedly reenters.)*

MARIA   *(following her to the brothel)* No, no, is it here? Is this it? *(The door closes in her face.)* This must be it!

---

7. "Oh, it's a woman. What do you want, you tart? Madam, come see."
8. A Bawd and a Madam are essentially the same figure, but in the original text Bontempelli specifies them with two different titles: the Ruffiana and the Padrona. Here it seems fair to consider the Bawd as a sort of assistant to the Madam.
9. "But, someone needs to call the police."

Massimo Bontempelli

Quickly and fearfully MARIA *moves away, looking toward the windows. A* SECOND PASSER-BY *enters from the right, singing under his breath.* MARIA *turns to him.*

SECOND PASSER-BY   Good evening.

MARIA   *(relieved)* Good evening, sir.

SECOND PASSER-BY   Very pretty. Let me get a good look.

MARIA   I need some information from you.

SECOND PASSER-BY   Let's see. *(He puts an arm around her and draws her under the red lamp.)* Sure. I'll give it to you. Come with me. I'm staying nearby. And you?

MARIA   No no...after...I can't leave now.... You misunderstood, you don't know.... Listen, you who are so good, I see that, you must help me. *(He steps aside, a bit taken aback.* MARIA *grabs him.)* I'm only here by chance —

SECOND PASSER-BY   *(freeing himself)* What's this? No, no!

MARIA   *(holding him back)* It's years and years that I've been traveling to find a place.... I think this is it, right here. Listen *(whispering)*, later I will tell you a secret. But now, you must help me.

A whistle from down the alley.

SECOND PASSER-BY   *(frightened)* The police! For goodness sake! Go on, go. I don't want any trouble.

SECOND PASSER-BY *forcefully pushes* MARIA *away. A clamor from the other side of the alley: two screaming* WOMEN *enter and run off to the left.*

MARIA   No, listen. Listen to me...

The SECOND PASSER-BY *hurries down the alley. Two* POLICEMEN *run in and seize* MARIA.

FIRST POLICEMAN   You're coming with us!

MARIA   *(struggling)* No, no, you're mistaken. I beg you, listen to me a minute.

SECOND POLICEMAN   Yes, yes, we'll get to that. Meanwhile, "march."

COURTESAN   *(appears)* Prenez-lá, prenez-lá, elle est une voleuse.[10]

---

10.   "Take her. Take her. She's a thief."

MARIA It's not true! It's not true! I'm a foreign lady. Let me explain.

FIRST POLICEMAN Please come with us, foreign lady. We'll show you a beautiful hotel.

MARIA *(struggling, screams)* No! No! I don't want to go. I can't leave here!

SECOND POLICEMAN Damn! She's a strong one, this…

FIRST POLICEMAN …foreign lady.

SOME MEN *(coming out of the tavern)* What was that? What's this? Oh! A little catch!

INNKEEPER *(behind them)* The question from before! A nocturnal tumult of human questions.

MARIA *(still screaming)* Let me go. Just a minute.

MADAM *(appears)* It's truly indecent! We have to change neighborhoods. These policemen don't know how to do their duty.

FIRST POLICEMAN Listen to that. The House of the Moon needs a more refined neighborhood.

MARIA The house of the moon! The house of the moon! She's there! She's in there!

TWO OR THREE OTHER CUSTOMERS *(entering from the tavern)* Down with the police!

FIRST POLICEMAN *(with a look at the other)* It's getting out of hand. *(whistles)*

CUSTOMERS They're calling for backup! It's not worth it!

The CUSTOMERS rush off left.

INNKEEPER *(shouting after them)* The check! The check!

Meanwhile the windows of the brothel have become populated with disheveled heads, with nude and powdered shoulders, breasts and arms. Everyone is screaming. All the windows are wide open, and the house sparkles fantastically with white light.

MARIA *(whose screams overpower all the rest)* There's the light, the light! She's inside! They took my baby away from me! She's inside! Take me in there! That's why they didn't let me in!

Two OTHER POLICEMEN run in.

Massimo Bontempelli

NEW POLICEMAN   Hey, hey, we're here. What is it?

The screams from the brothel become deafening.

SECOND POLICEMAN   Silence! Or I close the house and put you all in jail!

They grow silent.

SECOND POLICEMAN   (*to the* NEW POLICEMEN) Go in, bar all the exits, call for backup and search the place. And you (*to* MARIA) come with us.

He motions to the FIRST POLICEMAN, *and they drag* MARIA *away.*

MARIA   I don't want to! I don't want to! My —

A POLICEMAN *puts a hand over her mouth, suffocating her scream, and the* POLICEMEN *drag her off, down the alley. The* OTHER POLICEMEN *enter the brothel. Movement at the windows and muffled screams throughout. In the distance,* MARIA *screams again, but the sound is immediately stifled. The scene goes black, then changes.*

Episode Five

A prison.

> MARIA *sleeps. A knock on the wall.* MARIA *turns in her sleep. Another knock.* MARIA *wakes up.*

MARIA   Ah…

MARIA *knocks on the wall.*

WOMAN'S VOICE   *(from the other side of the wall)* Good morning.

MARIA   Good morning to you.

VOICE   For me it truly is good. It's the last, you know? I leave tomorrow.

MARIA   I'm happy. Happy for you. For me, no. I'll be all alone. You've been good company to me all this time, really wonderful.

VOICE   And how much longer must you stay?

MARIA   A month.

VOICE   It will pass. With God's help it will pass.

MARIA   Of course.

VOICE   And then where will you go?

MARIA   I don't know.

VOICE   You don't know?

MARIA   I know where I must go. But I don't yet know where that is, and I can't explain. I'm sorry.

VOICE   I'm going home, right away.

MARIA   Is it far from here?

VOICE   No. When you are free, will you come visit me?

MARIA   Maybe.

VOICE   I'll write the address for you. It's nearby. From town it's two hours by train then up toward the mountain. I come from the Moon towns.

MARIA   *(jumping up, shocked)* What did you say?

VOICE   It's a joke. Because the mountain is really, really high. There's snow there six months a year. In the summer, mountain climbers come. There are hotels in the foothills of my mountain, in the summer the rich people come. It's as cold as the city in the fall. And my village is still further up.

MARIA   Way, way up? In the peaks?

VOICE   Not quite. No one goes to the peaks, only the hunters. The village is called Three Peaks, precisely because there are three very tall mountain-peaks: High Peak, Cold Peak and Split Peak.

MARIA   Those are strange names.

VOICE   Split Peak, because it is cut in two, lengthwise, like two long, sharp teeth. There's a story in my village about that peak.

MARIA   What is the story?

VOICE   They say that it's the highest village on earth, that it's the first village where the light of the moon arrives.

MARIA   What? What? Describe it to me.

VOICE   When the mountain was all one piece, the light of the moon didn't reach the earth, and the night was really dark, and there was a lot of crime. So God ordered the moon to light up the earth at night.

MARIA   *(wailing)* No, no, not God!

VOICE   What's that you say?

MARIA   I'm sorry. Tell me. Tell me everything, I beg you. I like your story. *(listening intently)*

VOICE   And the moon lit up and sent her great light down over the earth. But the light struck against the mountains that closed off the pass.[11] So, to obey God's command, the moon, which had burning hot rays like the sun, began to beat against the mountain peaks, to break them. In the middle the mountain was made of a softer rock that breaks more easily. In fact the moon used up all these rays, pointlessly, on High Peak and Cold Peak, but on the peak in the middle she was able, little by little, to make a fissure and bit by bit to widen it and open it, like it is today. You will see it, if you come.

MARIA   I'll see it, for sure.

---

11.   Here once again, the term "light" is the masculine "lume" in the original text.

VOICE   And in fact the moon rises beyond that mountain peak, and the first light passes through that crack and comes over my village and then over the whole world.

MARIA   Over the whole world.

VOICE   But in that effort the moon used up all her might, and so she is much weaker than the sun. And so, because she is so feeble, every month she must rest for an entire week before she recovers a little strength and a little light to be able to return to the world.

MARIA   *(very anxious)* Does your village's story say anything else?

VOICE   No. They say that if the rock had resisted for a while longer, the moon would have used herself up completely. But because it was God who commanded her to arrive on earth, she was able to finish the job, and now she lights up the earth at night, by the will of God. *(pause)* Will you come visit me in my village?

MARIA   I will come, I will…after. That's enough for now.

VOICE   Don't you feel well?

MARIA   I'm fine.… No, that's not true. My head hurts, maybe. I got tired listening and talking like this, against the wall.

VOICE   Rest, you poor dear.

MARIA   Yes. I want to sleep a little. Excuse me.

VOICE   Sleep. Sleep is the prisoner's friend.

Pause.

MARIA   *(She collects her thoughts, murmuring.)* Between High Peak and Cold Peak, the Split Peak.… One month.…

The scene goes black, then changes.

Massimo Bontempelli

Episode Six

A room in a high mountain hotel. A terrace upstage toward the left.

The FRIEND *enters from the right. A* BELLMAN *passes.*

FRIEND There's no one here yet?

BELLMAN No, sir.

The BELLMAN *exits. Enter* MARIA *from the left.*

MARIA It's you!

FRIEND *(looking at her perplexed, then astonished)* Who?... Maria?!

MARIA Yes.

FRIEND Why?... How?

MARIA *(elated)* It's God. God has made it so that I run into you today, today, after many years. Don't be afraid. Now I understand destiny. My seeing you now — right now — was crucial. It's the sign —

FRIEND Now?

MARIA Don't ask me. You can't understand. Oh, there is one thing I want to tell you. (But don't be afraid of me. Tomorrow I'll vanish, maybe.) You don't know anything. I know everything. I have known the whole world, at its heights, in its depths. One more peak....

FRIEND Maria, and you, and you...have forgiven me?

MARIA Don't talk like that. Everything changes and becomes nobler.

FRIEND But the other...child?

MARIA Yes. The baby. She's far away, now. Don't think about it. One thing, yes, I want to say. When the baby should have died — she was so sick — I made a vow for you: the vow to meet you one day — it's today, you understand? — and to do something good for you, once. And so the baby got better. Then...but it's not important.... And I must do right by you, to keep my vow, before...

FRIEND Maria, I don't understand.

MARIA It's a strange thing, and great.

Enter a ROMANTIC GIRL *from the right.*

Watching the Moon

ROMANTIC GIRL *(astonished)* Aren't you coming to the terrace? Tonight there's a full moon. It's really beautiful, when it rises from Split Peak, just barely, little by little, and then manages to burst through and flood the whole valley.

MARIA The moon comes from heaven through Split Peak to the world.

ROMANTIC GIRL *(astonished)* Oh, it's true, ma'am. It really seems like it comes from there, first for us and then for the rest of the world.

FRIEND Shall we go?

MARIA *(sharply)* No.

ROMANTIC GIRL *(to him)* You're waiting for your girlfriend, I know. *(moving toward the terrace)* The valley will still be in shadow for a few more minutes. *(She exits.)*

MARIA *(with her face in her hands)* This is awful!

FRIEND It's late.

MARIA Is it cold?

FRIEND Maria!

A COUPLE *passes and goes to the terrace.*

MARIA *(still with her face in her hands)* I can't imagine going there.

FRIEND What is it? What are you thinking about?

MARIA *(Pause. She lifts her face, perturbed, but alight with joy.)* I'm thinking about tomorrow.

FRIEND *(shaken and perplexed)* You're scaring me. *(looking to the right)* It's her.

Enter, from the right, the GIRLFRIEND. MARIA *finds herself a bit apart, dazed.*

GIRLFRIEND *(to him)* Come on.

FRIEND *(hesitating)* Here I am.

GIRLFRIEND *takes his arm and pulls him toward the terrace, which is becoming lit by the moon.*

MARIA *(howling insanely)* No! No! Don't go. Everyone else yes, but you, no. He and you, no! I beg you. I command you.

GIRLFRIEND Ma'am…

FRIEND Just a minute…

MARIA *(without interruption)* I want it, want you to be saved. Stay here, stay here, for tonight. It's the last. *(She pushes them toward the exit on the right.)* Don't ask why. It's me who saves you.

FRIEND *(resolutely to the* GIRLFRIEND, *who tries to speak)* Come, come on. Later —

MARIA *(With an altered voice and violent gestures, she silences them and impedes their every movement. She pushes them inside.)* The vow is accomplished…now to free the world.

The BELLMAN *arrives from the left.* MARIA *turns toward him, still barring the right exit. Before he can speak, she inundates him with her agitated questions.*

MARIA How long does it take to climb up to Split Peak?

BELLMAN To Split Peak?

MARIA Yes, yes, answer me. Now!

BELLMAN About six hours, ma'am. People usually leave very early in the morning, first on mule, then on foot, and arrive at about two or three in the afternoon at the foot of Split Peak. At the shelter, you know.

MARIA On foot! And then?

BELLMAN Then?

MARIA Then? Further up.

BELLMAN You don't go further up. No one goes there. A few hunters, a few climbers.

MARIA Tomorrow morning wake me at four.

The BELLMAN *bows and exits.*

MARIA *(halts a moment, in the middle of the scene, immobile, as if gathering all her thoughts and all her strength; then she turns toward the window of the balcony and points to the sky, confident and defiant)* And for you, this is the last night. You can say goodbye to the earth. The earth is saved.

The scene goes black, then changes.

Watching the Moon

Episode Seven

The three peaks: High Peak, Cold Peak and in the middle Split Peak, as described by the prisoner in episode five.

Ten seconds of silence and immobility. Then a very distant chiming, which stops immediately. Silence again. MARIA *appears, crawling around the summit of a promontory of Split Peak, ragged and bloody with a crazed look. She peers below for a moment, menacing and gloomy, toward a point that remains hidden behind the rocks.*

VOICE *(from that direction, far in the distance)* Hey! Come down, if you can.

ANOTHER VOICE   No, stop. We'll try to come help you.

MARIA *(rasping, crazy)* Get away! Get away! I'll throw rocks at you!

VOICE   No! No! Just a minute! Let us come up!

MARIA *(almost roaring)* No…. *(rabidly grabbing big pieces of stone and rolling them down)* Get away! *(She doesn't move. We hear the rocks rolling, then shouts of fright and pain; then more rolling, then silence. Pathetically, she tries to climb again, groaning.)* Ow… ow…. *(She arrives at the base of the fissure and sinks in a torturous ravine of rock. She shivers.)* It's cold. Where am I cold? *(She squeezes her legs.)* I don't feel them, I don't feel them, if they are still there…. *(shivers again)* It burns…. Will she come? *(She leans with difficulty toward the opening in the rock. To the left, a weak glimmer begins to illuminate the little sky seen beyond the peaks)* Is she coming? Is it her?… Ah!…

With a superhuman effort MARIA *manages to lift herself a little and straighten up right in the middle of the fissure, as if stuck inside it.*

MARIA   Come on! Hurry! Before I die I want to get a hold of you, you wicked thing. I want you to give back what you've stolen from me. Ah, come on, come on! *(The glimmer grows and moves from the left toward the center.)* It's your last night. You'll never arrive on the earth again. You'll die. I know, I know that I can't get to you, you thief, but I will die, here, tight like this. I'll become mountain, and you won't be able to pass through me, ever again…. Come on, don't you have the guts? Ah, that's right! That's right! Me and you!

Massimo Bontempelli

The moonlight invests her entirely, and projects her shadow all the way downstage. MARIA *fumbles with her arms up high toward the light: she shivers even more.*

MARIA   You want to kill me with your cold? Yes, kill me, but just try and pass, if you can. I've vanquished you.

MARIA's *shadow grows bigger, mixing with the shadows of the peaks and the nearby spires. The very figure of* MARIA *is muddled with them and seems to stiffen and lose its form.*

MARIA   *(with a fiery, distant voice)* Little one, my little one, where are you?... I can't come.... But I've...avenged you.... I've... saved... the world...the mothers who remain...alone...in the world....

MARIA's *silhouette is lost in the confusion and deformation of the shadows. All we see is a mix of peaks, of splinters, of spires.*

MARIA   *(barely audible)* My little one....

Ten seconds of total and immobile silence.

The End

Stormcloud

A Play

Massimo Bontempelli

A Note on the Text

I've translated *Nembo* from the 1947 volume, *Teatro* I (Milan: Mondadori), whose only modification to the 1936 text (Rome: Edizioni di Novissima) is the correction of a typographical error. Written in January of 1935, the play received a handful of radio broadcasts between 1938 and 1942 but was performed in the theater only toward the end of Bontempelli's life, despite initial plans by Anton Giulio Bragaglia to produce it at the government-sponsored Teatro delle Arti. Bontempelli himself had expressed doubts that the Italian theater — with still limited technical capabilities — was ready for the piece and expected that, in any case, only a very small audience would appreciate it. (This is particularly interesting since at the time Bontempelli championed theater for the masses.) The play would have to wait for Vito Pandolfi, one of the brightest theatrical talents of the postwar generation, to direct it in 1958. Bontempelli didn't write music especially for the play, but he published some pieces that he had already written and found particularly apt, suggesting that arrangements be unimposing and for just a few instruments.

A couple of key words are important for analyzing the play; the first of these is its title, *Nembo*. A *nembo* is a nimbus or a rain cloud, but it seemed to me that the danger the cloud brings with it was better expressed with "stormcloud." Most interesting, however, is that the word *nembo* may also be used to refer to a mass of people — as observed in the introduction, the danger of the masses was one of the author's concerns. Other key words are the male characters' names, Felice (which means "happy") and Marzio (which means "martial," deriving from Mars). Early in the play, the significance of these names seems appropriate and even transparent — Felice is cheerful and a lover of life and games, while Marzio discusses the need for order, urges Regina to be more serious and tends to be rather brusque, with a gloom that perhaps promises violence. But then things change. I've opted to leave the names as-is in the text, but for ease of pronunciation in performance, equivalents could of course be used: Felice, a common name in Italian even today, easily becomes Felix. Marzio is far less common, and sounds distinctly (ancient) Roman: an appropriate equivalent, then, may be a name like Martius, rather than more common derivatives like Martin, or Marcus, and is especially preferable to a name like Mark, which recalls the Judeo-Christian tradition — certainly not the resonance of the war-related Marzio.

On the other names, it's worth noting that Regina isn't a very common name in Italian. It means "queen" and therefore functions as a title. I've also left the children's names as-is in the text: Fulvia, Sesto, Tino and Milla (the last two of which can easily remain unaltered). Fulvia derives from the Latin "fulvus," which means dusky, tawny or a sort of a red-yellow. Names with a meaning that come close could be Tawny or even a nick-namey solution like "Blondie." However, these lose the "high" nature of Fulvia, which is a rather aristocratic Roman name — Marc Antony's wife was named Fulvia. To the Italian ear, "Tino" sounds like a short version for some name: Antonino? Santino? Also noteworthy is the diminutive "ino." Sesto's literal meaning is "sixth," as for the sixth born (though the text doesn't seem to indicate that Sesto and Tino have other siblings). True English equivalents for Sesto are in reality Latin: Sextus and Sixtus (the name of five popes), but the uncommon Sesto probably requires a more modest, similar-sounding name in English.

P.G.

Massimo Bontempelli

Characters

REGINA, MARZIO, AND FELICE: YOUNG PEOPLE

FULVIA, MILLA, TINO, SESTO AND OTHER CHILDREN

MOTHERS

THE ORATOR

THE CARETAKER

THE ATTENDANT

THE LEADER

POLICEMEN

MEN AND WOMEN

Episode One

A large green meadow without a tree in sight and in the distance the azure sky without a cloud. On the right, a glaringly white wall, cut off by the beginning of a road, indicates that we are at the furthest city limits.

In the middle of the meadow the children have marked a square for playing "Puss in a Corner." Four round sticks are stuck in the ground at the corners; leaning on each is its hoop. The children are FULVIA, TINO, SESTO, *and* MILLA *(between six and eight years old; Milla is the smallest). They play noisily with* REGINA *(who is nineteen).* REGINA *is currently in the middle. The* CHILDREN *exchange places around her, shouting joyfully.* REGINA *begins to run towards one spot; when she realizes she won't make it, she goes for another, but doesn't make it to any of them.*

FULVIA   With us you can't make it!

FOUR CHILDREN   *(in unison)* You can't make it!

TINO   *(behind* REGINA'*s back, signals to* MILLA*)* Here, Milla, here!

TINO *and* MILLA *change places.*

FULVIA   *(running, to* SESTO*)* Don't get caught, you dummy!

SESTO   *(running, to* REGINA*)* Pay attention!

REGINA   You bumped into me. That's not fair.

SESTO   Aw, she doesn't know: the rules are, there are no rules!

Scene design for *Stormcloud*, Episode One, by H. Blaettler. The Getty Research Institute, Los Angeles (910147).

FOUR CHILDREN   She doesn't know anything, doesn't know anything.

TINO   (*to* SESTO) Run.

MILLA   Nobody looks at me.

SESTO   (*to* MILLA) Go.

SESTO *runs toward* MILLA, *but sees that* REGINA *runs up, so he turns right around.* MILLA *shouts joyfully as she runs toward him, but* REGINA *gets the place.*

MILLA   No, no… (*She stands there for a moment and then begins to cry.*)

Noise and shouting.

TINO and FULVIA   (*making fun of* MILLA) Uh…Uh….

SESTO   What a twit!

REGINA   (*runs to* MILLA *and hugs her*) No, no, it was just for fun. It doesn't count. Run there. (*She pushes* MILLA *toward the space she has left free.*)

TINO   No, that's not allowed!

SESTO   You're ruining the game!

FULVIA   Cheaters![1]

SESTO   Milla in the middle! Milla in the middle!

MILLA   No, no. I'm not moving ever again.

FULVIA   Then there's no game.

TINO   (*to* MILLA) You don't know how to play. Get lost.

REGINA   But, no. She's little.

MILLA   That's not true. I'm almost as big as the others.

FULVIA   Milla is too little to play with us.

SESTO   And Regina is too big.

MARZIO   (*appears down the street on the right and calls*) Regina.

---

1. In the original text Fulvia actually says, "Fate la camorra," accusing them of acting like mobsters for breaking the rules or taking unfair control of the game. (The Camorra is Naples' organized crime network.)

Stormcloud

REGINA *(turning towards him)* Good morning, Marzio.

TINO But Regina…

FULVIA Pay attention. Play!

MILLA Here, Tino, here.

SESTO Ignore that guy. You're playing with us.

MARZIO *(advances on the children, sternly)* That's enough. Leave her be. She needs to talk to me. Regina, a little order. I sent you word that I wanted to talk. You said I would find you here, and here I find you — playing. But what I have to say to you is no game.

REGINA *(to the* CHILDREN*)* Let's rest a minute, then we'll play again.

The CHILDREN, *grumbling, stop playing.*

SESTO Where's the fun in that?

FULVIA It was just getting started.

TINO It's always like this when the grown-ups play.

FULVIA Now what do we do?

REGINA *and* MARZIO, *side by side, stroll slowly downstage.*

SESTO What do you think? We've got the hoops.

TINO This was mine.

TINO *tears the stick from the ground and uses it to push the hoop upstage. The others do the same.* MILLA, *too, picks up the hoop and stick, but then, after pushing the hoop just a few steps, she stops.*

MILLA I'm tired. *(flops down on the grass, off to the side downstage)*

SESTO *(running again)* Those two are playing the lovebirds, hey? Yuck.

FULVIA *laughs stupidly.*

  During the dialogue that follows, between REGINA *and* MARZIO *at the proscenium,* SESTO, FULVIA, *and* TINO *continue to run around with the hoops, all over the stage.* REGINA *and* MARZIO *have stopped. She looks at him expectantly.*

REGINA *(after a brief hesitation, teasing him a bit)* You can do it, Marzio.

MARZIO Don't act that way. Sometimes I wonder if you are serious.

REGINA Do we have to be serious?

MARZIO Yes. Life is a very serious thing.

REGINA I am not life.

MARZIO Every one of us is life, always for ourselves, sometimes for another. You could be my life, my whole life. I told you once before.

REGINA No, twice. This is the third time.

MARZIO Even better. And every time I talk to you, I'm disappointed, which should push me away. But when you leave, despite the disappointment, I feel a little bit more attached to you. Explain this to me.

REGINA You have this obsession that everything can be explained.

MARZIO At least one should try.

REGINA The most beautiful things are those we don't understood.

MARZIO Words. Don't change the subject. I want to marry you. There — that explains everything.

REGINA Is that right? Then I can go back to the game. *(makes as if to move)*

MARZIO *(holding her back)* No. It's not enough that I want to marry you.

REGINA That's very true. I would also have to want to marry you.

MARZIO And so, so you can decide —

REGINA God, decide.

MARZIO For you to want it, too, you need to know what I can give you. So much. If you loved me, I could give you everything one could ever want in life. I —

REGINA But, my dear, if I loved you, and you love me, there's no need to give me anything else. Nothing else matters.

MARZIO How do you know? You are nineteen years old.

REGINA That's a lot of years.

MARZIO I don't know. It could also be not very many at all.

Stormcloud

REGINA In that case, let's wait until I'm older. How old? Twenty? Forty?

MARZIO There you go — playing again.

REGINA I'm being prudent.

MARZIO What is that supposed to mean?

REGINA I'll explain it to you. Eight years ago — you hadn't come to our town yet — I had a little sister. She was seven. One day, beautiful, like this, she was in a meadow, like this one. She ran around like these kids now.... *(She turns to look and notices that* MILLA *sits on the ground away from the others, who run around.)* What is it, Milla? Why aren't you running with the others?

MILLA Oh, first I was tired, then I forgot. Yes, yes. *(She gets up.)* Come with us?

REGINA Soon, Milla.

MILLA *runs to join the other children.*

MARZIO So, Regina?

REGINA What were we saying? Were we done?

MARZIO You make me miserable. Are you doing it on purpose?

REGINA No. I never do anything on purpose.

MARZIO Now that is a terrible confession. You had started to tell me about a little sister.

REGINA She was running around like those kids. The nanny came to call her because it was time for grammar lessons, and she began to cry. She said, "just a little longer," but no, they took her home. Then the stormcloud arrived, the terrible stormcloud of our town. You have no —

MARZIO They told me about it.

REGINA But you never saw it. You have no idea. The stormcloud that suddenly arrives in the sky, from who knows where, and rains death all over our town. It only kills children, lots of them, in an hour, in ten minutes. It's horrendous — nothing can be done about it — then it disappears and returns who knows when, after ten years, after a hundred, without any warning, like volcanoes in other places. That was it. That was the last one.

An hour later, the little one was dead. She died studying her grammar. Wouldn't it have been better if she had died chasing her hoop?

MARZIO   Regina, I already told you not to change the subject. My deep love, the quiet and beautiful future that I offer your life… what is it?

He is interrupted because the CHILDREN *begin to scream more loudly, happily, running in a group toward the corner upstage on the left.*

FULVIA   *(running with the others, she turns a moment toward* REGINA *and shouts to her)* Felice's here, come here!

SESTO   Your other boyfriend.

FULVIA   *(to* MARZIO*)* Are you jealous?

MILLA   Jealous, jealous.…

REGINA   Tell Felice to come here.

MARZIO   They said it: the other one. Be honest. You're in love with Felice.

REGINA   No, for now neither with him nor with you. It's a pity. If I were in love with one of you, it would be so easy. But as it is.…

MARZIO   As it is, because of your unbelievable innocence, neither of us.… But I love you more — I love you better. No, I'm the one who truly loves you, Regina, as one should love.

REGINA   As one should love? And how do you know that?

FELICE *arrives from the corner upstage left, surrounded by the* CHILDREN. *They come forward in a group, shouting.* REGINA *goes to meet them.*

CHILDREN   Regina, let's play. Regina, come back.

FELICE   I want to play, too.

TINO   Play what?

MILLA   "Puss in the Corner" again. I was never in the middle.

TINO   Yes, yes, you were!

SESTO   But we can't play with six.

FULVIA   If we can play with four places for five, we can play with five places for six.

Stormcloud

The CHILDREN *begin to plant the poles back in the ground.*

REGINA We're missing a pole. How can we mark the fifth spot?

TINO See, it's useless. We can't.

SESTO Let's change games.

FELICE That's it, Regina. Changing the game — that's what life is.

MARZIO *has withdrawn upstage as if to leave, but slows his pace, and every once in a while turns to watch them, without resolving to leave.*

TINO Let's play "Cops and Robbers."

FULVIA There's not enough of us.

SESTO How about "Hide and Seek"?

REGINA But no. Put the pole here, put the hoop here, and there, the fifth spot is made. *(She does it.)*

FELICE See? There's a remedy for everything.

CHILDREN Yes, that's good. Who's in the middle?

SESTO We have to do the count.

REGINA Felice is in the middle.

FELICE *goes to the middle, and they start the game.*

FELICE *(still following the game)* Regina, I want us to get married and have twelve children. Then we can play any game.

SESTO Run, Regina!

SESTO *and* REGINA *run to exchange places, but* FELICE *takes* REGINA*'s.*

REGINA *(in the middle)* Mr. Bossy! Is that how you make serious proposals to me?

TINO *(to* FULVIA*)* Here, here.

TINO *and* FULVIA *change places.*

MILLA And me?

FELICE Here, Milla.

FELICE *and* MILLA *change places.*

FELICE But I didn't make all these serious proposals. I proposed that we get married.

SESTO *(slowing his run)* Look, meanwhile they're playing husband and wife!

TINO Enough chatter! Pay attention, Fulvia. *(They run.)*

REGINA Marriage is the most serious thing there is.

FELICE No, it's the most beautiful.

SESTO runs toward TINO, but TINO, tired, isn't paying attention, and FELICE takes SESTO's place.

SESTO *(angry, to TINO)* Ah, your fault!

FELICE Regina, we are a beautiful couple, and we will make a beautiful life.... There, there, Fulvia!

FULVIA *(tries to move, but is tired)* I can't do it anymore.

TINO Me neither.

REGINA Oh God! What is it?

Suddenly the CHILDREN seem weak. Their movement becomes slow and limp, almost like a slow-motion film scene. A far off clamor of frightened and confused howling.

MILLA *(wailing)* Mama, mama.

REGINA *(alarmed)* Felice, Marzio.

FELICE and MARZIO run to her. The air around them goes dark as a leaden cloud appears high in the sky.

MARZIO *(as if to comfort)* Shh, Regina.

REGINA *(desperate)* Like before.

FELICE We're here.

REGINA The children...it's the stormcloud.

The clamor from the city nears. The CHILDREN, clinging to one another, come to REGINA, MARZIO and FELICE. Moaning, they fall at their feet.

FELICE It's nothing, sweeties. Come on, Milla. *(takes MILLA in his arms)*

MARZIO It's passing. Let's go home. *(takes SESTO and TINO)*

REGINA Fulvia, don't be afraid.

FULVIA I'm really afraid!

Stormcloud

MILLA *(knocking about in* FELICE*'s arms)* Don't hold me so tight.

REGINA *(with one arm around* FULVIA*)* Milla, be good. We're going to your mama. Don't be afraid.

MILLA No, I don't want to.

MILLA *hits* FELICE, *escapes and runs like mad toward the city, offstage to the right.*

REGINA *(handing* FULVIA *to* MARZIO, *she runs after* MILLA*)* Wait for me here, you two. Milla, Milla!

REGINA, *chasing after* MILLA, *vanishes.*

The darkness increases. PEOPLE *in delirium invade the stage. A* MOTHER *breaks off from the people and runs to* FULVIA.

FULVIA'S MOTHER You're here. You're alive.

FULVIA'S MOTHER *takes* FULVIA *in her arms and runs away.* ANOTHER MOTHER *breaks off from the crowd.*

SESTO AND TINO'S MOTHER *(running to them)* Sesto, Tino… *(She takes* SESTO *and* TINO *in her arms, and they run. After a few steps, they fall to the ground, and she throws herself over the boys, sobbing.)* No, no, my babies. Let's go home. *(but she is unable to move them)*

A group of MEN *and* WOMEN *arrive, carrying and holding* CHILDREN *by the hand. One is at the head of the group, as if leading them. They run toward the left where there is open country.*

LEADER Follow me, quickly! Maybe it won't catch us.

But the stormcloud slowly shifts toward the left in the sky. The GROUP, *behind the* LEADER, *disappears to the left.* TWO POLICEMEN *come down the street.*

POLICEMAN Everyone go home. That's an order. Shut yourselves inside immediately. Go home. Go home. And be calm, be calm. That's the order.

The TWO POLICEMEN *try to push people toward the street.* SESTO *and* TINO'S MOTHER *now manages to take* SESTO *and* TINO *away.* ANOTHER WOMAN *runs in from the left.*

WOMAN Milla! Milla was supposed to be here. Where is she?

FELICE She ran home, ma'am. That way. She was with Regina.

WOMAN   *(runs off down the street, shouting like a person possessed)* Milla…

The scene clears. The noise becomes distant and faint. Silence. In the silence, MARZIO *and* FELICE *draw near to one another. They look intensely at one another. Pause.*

MARZIO   Just like that, in an instant, the world becomes another.

FELICE   Another, outside and in.

MARZIO   Felice, I didn't hate you.

FELICE   I know. Let's go to Regina.

MARZIO   *(putting a hand on* FELICE*'s shoulder to hold him back)* No. She told us to wait for her here.

FELICE   You and I together…it's strange.

MARZIO   All those children, maybe they're already dead.

FELICE   It's vile.

MARZIO   Could Regina die too?

FELICE   *(with a scream)* No! *(seeking to convince himself, murmurs)* This scourge only kills children…almost… *(stammering, he's so overcome)* and Regina…Regina.

MARZIO   She's not a child, I think.[2] Calm down, Felice. Why does the idea that Regina could die upset you so much?

FELICE   *(astonished)* Well — because I love her.

MARZIO   And I don't love her, you think? No?

FELICE   *(looks at him)* I know. It's true. And so why aren't you crazy with fear?

MARZIO   *(shaking his head)* That's got nothing to do with it.

FELICE   But the thing that matters most…

MARZIO   The thing that matters most is to know how to love, is to love as much as you can, *(raising his voice)* is loving as nobly

---

2.   The rather strange structure of this line — it's not a simple "I don't think she's a child" — may suggest that Marzio isn't discussing Regina's age or childlike nature but instead a medical fact: that, menstruation having begun, she is no longer a child. The "I think" then clarifies that he does not in fact know such an intimate thing about her.

as you can. *(lowering his tone)* And we can love a person who is dead more nobly, Felice.

FELICE *(remains struck as if he doesn't understand, then is suddenly afraid to have understood)* But that's — awful — an egotism —

MARZIO The most awful egotism is always love.

FELICE No, no. I'm so afraid.

MARZIO Afraid of a word.

FELICE *(Restless, he looks around.)* Why isn't she coming back?

MARZIO She will. There she is.

REGINA *appears down the street. She is transfigured by compassion and fatigue. She comes forward, leaning against the white wall.*

REGINA I promised I'd come back. It's awful, there. *(indicating the city)* Life is turned upside down. Milla too.... But I promised I'd come back. Perhaps you were arguing over which of you loves me the most.

MARZIO No, Regina.

FELICE Only for a minute.

REGINA That's a long time. As for me, from the depths of my heart, I tell you, my dears, that I don't know. I don't know. And the thing grows distant. But I'd like you to forgive me.

MARZIO *(dismayed)* Forgive you for what, Regina?

FELICE No, no. Why are you talking this way?

REGINA To forgive me and to stop tiring yourselves out thinking about it.... There's a little bit of light. The stormcloud is going away. *(In fact, the air and the sky are clearing up.)* I was saying, don't tire yourselves out over this — who loves me more — because I think, Felice, I think, Marzio, no, I'm sure...it's no use, because...because...once more I ask you...from the bottom of my heart...forgiveness.

Her back leaning against the wall, REGINA *slides down to the ground. She slumps over a little, as if dead.*

FELICE *(shouting)* No! It can't be! *(He kneels over her.)*

MARZIO *(similarly kneeling over her)* You, too, Regina, little child....

Massimo Bontempelli

FELICE *and* MARZIO *sit on the ground near* REGINA*'s body. They each begin to take one of her hands, but they don't dare. At the farthest point upstage, from the city toward the open country, an exodus begins: an exodus of disheartened and changed* PEOPLE, *with bundles and sacks on their shoulders, with inert children in their arms. The cloud has passed, but the sky is left dirty, in tatters.*

Stormcloud

Episode Two

The corner of a courtyard surrounded by a colonnade. Upstage, two segments of the colonnade come together at a right angle, which diagonally enclose the scene. The long segment is on the left. In it are three short, wide doors, covered by heavy curtains. In the short segment, on the right, another opening similarly protected by a curtain. The main entrance is at the beginning of the longest side and therefore at the farthest point downstage left. At the vertex of the right angle of the colonnade, just downstage and therefore in the courtyard just in front of the colonnade, a low statue in a rather funerary style, very simple. It's late at night. The scene is dimly lit by lamps hidden behind the cornice of the colonnade.

On the step at the base of the statue's pedestal, the Orator *is finishing speaking. Throughout the courtyard, spiritless and sleepy people listen, indifferently, to the end of the speech. The* Caretaker *and the* Attendant *keep watch.*

Orator   (*Every once in a while he thinks a phrase, then says it.*) And now, my friends, tried by grief, return calmly to your homes. Death must not interrupt life. There is something more important than individual feelings…even more sacred than each of us…than us small men. (*He thinks.*) Think that your children died in innocence, with the smile of childhood on their lips. And think that if the world of life is painful because we know it — death — therefore to not know it is certainly a world of superior joy…where your children wait for you…from where they look over you, to see that you are at peace. (*He thinks.*) The mysterious calamity that every so often falls upon our innocent town… (*He thinks.*) is not a misfortune, if we accept it with steadfastness, like a power greater than us… (*He thinks.*) and therefore better, you understand? And more just. (*Pause. Changes tone.*) Enough. Now those of you who have seen your children for the last time, go to sleep, and tomorrow morning calmly take up your work. This is the order, and we must obey. Those who are still inside (*He turns to the door, to the* Caretaker *and the* Attendant.) have to clear out right away, because it's time to

Scene design for *Stormcloud*, Episode Two, by H. Blaettler. The Getty Research Institute, Los Angeles (910147).

close. And to all of you, I repeat: death is the highest form of life. This is the order. Goodbye.³

The ORATOR *comes down the steps drying his face. He looks around a moment and, passing through the people with a low and ambiguous murmur, he leaves through the main exit on the right.*

WOMAN *(desolately)* It is so.

MILLA'S MOTHER No, it isn't so. *(screams)* My Milla, I want her! *(She throws herself toward one of the doors on the left.)*

CARETAKER *(putting his arms around* MILLA'S MOTHER*)* Be quiet, ma'am. Quiet. You know that I can't let anyone else in now.

ONE MAN ALONE My son too, ma'am, he was so beautiful.

MILLA'S MOTHER Milla is more beautiful. *(in the* CARETAKER*'s arms, calls)* Milla....

OLD MAN He said we have to be calm, because that's the order.

SECOND WOMAN *(sobbing)* But the one who gave the order, nobody died on him.

WORKER The Orator speaks because he is paid to speak. Like me, I'm a carpenter, and I make tables because they pay me. So he does what he must, like me.

SECOND WOMAN *(obstinate)* But if he had lost someone, his own child?

WORKER *(explaining)* Then they would have paid someone else to speak.

A COUPLE *comes out of one of the doors on the left.*

HE *(trying to console her)* We'll have another one soon. The first one born, you'll see, it'll be like he's come back.

SHE It doesn't have to be this way.... It doesn't have to be this way....

They exit.

---

3. Given the setting at a funeral and the tenor of the speech, it seems safe to assume that the Orator is a priest. ("Orare" in fact means "to pray.") It's likely that Bontempelli refrained from labeling the character as such due to censorship regulations, which would have prohibited such an unflattering representation of the clergy.

Massimo Bontempelli

SESTO AND TINO'S MOTHER   For me, two. Both of them. None of you had two die. And I am a widow. None of you is a widow and lost two.

From one of those doors on the left, a SECOND COUPLE *enters.*

HE   *(brusquely)* Now, go back home. I'm not coming.

SHE   Why? Where are you going at this hour?

HE   I'm not coming home. Now that he's not here, there is no us.

SHE   *(bows her head)* All right.

HE *and* SHE *go.*

THIN WOMAN   *(Entering from another door on the left, she runs into a* MAN, *and attacks him.)* You? Here? You have the nerve?

MAN   I want to see our son.

THIN WOMAN   Since you left us, he's all mine. Go away.

MAN   In the face of death.

THIN WOMAN   In the face of death? I'll kill you.

VARIED VOICES   It's a disgrace — a bit of respect — at the door....

CARETAKER   *(intervening)* Go on, now, it's closed.

The CARETAKER *pushes the* MAN *and the* THIN WOMAN *out of the doorway. Others enter through the door, some led gently by the* CARETAKER, *others by the* ATTENDANT.

BOY   *(holding a* DAZED WOMAN'*s hand)* They didn't let me see anything. They saw everything, and I didn't.

DAZED WOMAN   Come, darling. *(She leads the* BOY *toward the exit.)*

BOY   *(going reluctantly)* But I want to see the dead people one more time.

DAZED WOMAN *and* BOY *exit.*

MAN WITH SALT AND PEPPER HAIR   *(from the corner directly opposite, screams)* What? Who is that? *(He pushes his way toward the exit.)* I heard a boy's voice. Why was there a boy here?

A WOMAN   He left.

MAN WITH SALT AND PEPPER HAIR   No, no. I heard him speak. Why did he speak? Because he was alive. It can't be! Mine is dead, and so many others. And I believed that all the children were dead, and so it was right if mine were too. But if even just one remains, it's no longer right. It's an abomination. *(growing more excited as a few others restrain him)* It can't be tolerated. Kill him. Let me go. I'll kill him myself. Where is he?

TWO COMPANIONS   *(One on each side, they hold him back.)* Come on, come on.

MAN WITH SALT AND PEPPER HAIR   Let go of me! I'll find him. If not, the rule no longer exists.[4] Let me go. Let's put things right. *(Shouting again, he breaks away from the two who keep hold of him.)*

WOMAN   And that one there *(indicating the exit of the portico on the right)* is the only adult who is dead. Nineteen, almost twenty. The others, they were all under ten. That's an injustice, too.

COMPANION   She was like a little girl, a little orphan. Alone in the world without a family.

A WOMAN *appears in the threshold and clings to it.*

CARETAKER   *(to the* WOMAN*)* Be brave — see, the others are leaving, too.

CLINGING WOMAN   Curse you, and curse the heavens.

YOUNG MAN   *(scandalized)* Don't say "Curse the heavens." It's not right.

The CLINGING WOMAN *and the* YOUNG MAN *exit.*

DEMAGOGUE   *(rabid)* Why "it's not right"? You're all sheep. And that other one, *(indicating the place where the* ORATOR *had been)* "Tomorrow morning you will take up your work again. That is the order." And so all of you, you sheep, go calmly because that's the order. "There is a decree to calmly accept death," and you accept it, and you leave! You need to rebel, sheep!

MARZIO *and* FELICE *enter through the main entrance.*

---

4.   This line is interesting particularly in light of another of Bontempelli's works, the novel *Gente nel tempo*. In that story, death comes to a given family every five years. The rule of destiny dictates that (usually premature) death is inevitable — it's merely a question of who will succumb. Here, the man accepts as a rule that the stormcloud will always come to town, but therefore expects that all of the children must die.

MARZIO   Rebel against the stormcloud from heaven? How? Who will be the leader? Who will finance it, this revolution against heaven?

DEMAGOGUE   *(dumbfounded)* Who are you?

MARZIO   It's not important. Away with you.

DEMAGOGUE   *(grumbling)* Sheep and philosophers. What a world!

Following all of the men and women, the DEMAGOGUE *exits. Only* MARZIO, FELICE, *the* CARETAKER *and the* ATTENDANT *remain.*

MARZIO   *(to the* CARETAKER, *who has approached him)* No one else is in there?

CARETAKER   No, there was the order to send everyone away.... Oh, I don't mean them.[5]

ATTENDANT   These gentlemen are only just arriving, and maybe....

MARZIO   Aren't they all children?

ATTENDANT   In there *(motioning to the left)* all children, and lots of them....

MARZIO   *(to* FELICE*)* So little, and they've already done something so important.

ATTENDANT   They'll be buried tomorrow at vespers. There was only one young woman. *(indicates the door with curtains under the arcade on the right)* They'll take her away the day after tomorrow, at early morning.

FELICE   *(pleading)* Let's go now to see her. It's for the last time, Marzio.

MARZIO   *(with firm kindness)* I'm not coming.

FELICE   *(through tears, looks at him, stupefied)* You, no? You said you loved her.

MARZIO   The one I love isn't in there. She lives in another place that is all around me, but also inside me. When the person we love lives, she cannot be all inside us like that. That's why every love for a living person is always full of restlessness and wanting.

FELICE   Because you didn't really love her.

---

5. An evident reference to the dead children.

Stormcloud

MARZIO   *(shaking his head with compassion)* When the living truly love their dead, they will destroy their cold bodies to the last molecule, scatter them. *(with growing passion)* They won't have cemeteries. They won't need tombs, nor a headstone nor an urn. Only then will the spirit world be able to violently embrace the world of the living, and give us the strength to live more peacefully. To keep a dead person's picture will be a horrendous sacrilege.

FELICE   But the grief, Marzio?

MARZIO   Grief doesn't matter. Grief is egotism full of satisfaction.

FELICE   I don't understand you. I love her. I want to see her.

MARZIO   Go.

The ATTENDANT *holds open the curtain of the door on the right. A soft glow from within.* FELICE *goes inside. The curtain falls closed behind him. Pause.* FELICE *sobs loudly, then stops.* FELICE *returns and throws himself onto* MARZIO, *putting his head on his shoulder. Almost immediately he straightens back up.*

MARZIO   Are you ready to go?

FELICE   And yet, you know? You feel better. Go see her.

MARZIO   No, I told you.

FELICE   It brings a sense of peace…she doesn't seem dead. It seems like she's sleeping. It's like when she was dying, remember? That day…no…but when was it? Oh, only this morning. There hasn't even been a revolution of the sun —

MARZIO   They say that life is short. If we measure it by our misfortunes, it could become terribly long.

FELICE   — since she wanted us to forgive her. What is there for us to forgive in that dear innocent creature?

MARZIO   Forgive her her innocence.

FELICE   And she thought that we were fighting over which of us loved her more. Would she have wanted to know, do you think?

MARZIO   Of course, to understand whom she herself could have loved better.

FELICE It's strange that even then we didn't feel like rivals. It was a presentiment. It's important.

MARZIO And it's very important that after the fact one always discovers a certain number of important presentiments.

FELICE *(turning toward that door)* Goodbye forever, Regina. *(to* MARZIO*)* To have seen her was a miracle for my soul… I don't know how to tell you. You won't go, I understand. But certainly, if she, from there, sees — I don't know. I don't have very clear ideas about these things — if from there she sees that you didn't go there to see her, she'll have no doubt which of us loved her more.

MARZIO *and* FELICE *begin to cross toward the exit.*

MARZIO But if from there she sees — I'm not very certain about this either — if from there she sees, it won't matter to her one bit.

The ATTENDANT *follows them in hopes of a tip, but* MARZIO *and* FELICE *exit. The* ATTENDANT *returns and lies down in front of the doors on the left, preparing to sleep.*

ATTENDANT Did you see?

CARETAKER What?

ATTENDANT They forgot about us. You did the right thing, staying where you were.

CARETAKER I'm not surprised. That's how they behave, the kind of people who reason so well about everything. Didn't you hear them? They reason, and they forget to act. I never reason, and I would never make the kind of impression that they did on us. It is the greatest vice of the century: to reason. Why reason? I've learned to find everything very simple. There's a branch, ok? Attached to the branch is a fruit, you see it? I take the fruit, put it in my mouth. I eat it, I am well. Being well, that's what matters. My wife makes a baby. It's natural. The baby falls ill, then dies. This too is natural. If it hadn't been born, it couldn't have died, therefore passing into life or passing on to death is the same thing. But being well and being ill are not the same thing. God has commanded us: seek to be well. Yes, Lord. And to be well, one has to sleep. *(The* ATTENDANT *begins to snore.)* Oh, you were already sleeping. So who I am talking for? Why let me talk and not tell me? You're sleeping there. I'll sleep here. Both of us in the starlight. Tomorrow evening each will sleep in his own bed. *(He looks up.)* So many stars. It's a shame that there is no switch to turn them out. But the stars aren't much of a nuisance. Good night.

Pause. Now the CARETAKER *also begins to snore, but quieter than the* ATTENDANT, *and in a higher pitch. A moaning comes from behind the curtain on the right. Pause, then another. Then the* CARETAKER's *snoring stops for a moment. From inside, a third moan, clearer, that morphs into a word. It's* REGINA's *voice.*

REGINA *(inside)* Milla…

The ATTENDANT's *snoring becomes heavy breathing that gradually turns silent.*

CARETAKER *(lifts his head, murmurs)* It seemed like… *(His head falls back down; he falls asleep again in silence.)*

REGINA *(inside)* Milla…Fulvia…Tino…Sesto… *(pause, then more clearly, as if she is picking herself up)* Felice, Marzio…

The CARETAKER *sits up and listens. Pause. The curtain sways, is pulled aside, and* REGINA *appears on the threshold.*

REGINA Where am I?

CARETAKER The girl! She was alive!

REGINA You thought I was dead? When did this happen? Where am I?

CARETAKER *(stands up)* If it were him, *(indicates the* ATTENDANT, *who continues to sleep peacefully)* at this hour, he would have screamed and run away.

REGINA Who's afraid?

CARETAKER Not me. That is the advantage of finding everything natural.

REGINA What do you find natural?

CARETAKER For example, it's natural that we believed you were dead. Anyway the living are always in a hurry to definitively organize their dead. And since you were not dead, it's natural that you have woken up and come to speak to me.

REGINA   Now I remember. My little friends…I went back to the meadow, because I had promised them. I spoke again with my older friends. After that, I don't remember.

CARETAKER   Don't strain yourself, it doesn't matter. Remembering is useless, like reasoning. What are your intentions?

REGINA   Intentions? I don't know. Now I am well.

CARETAKER   Ah, being well: the only thing that matters. I told him that, too, but he was sleeping.

REGINA   How strange. This place doesn't seem new to me. What is it?

CARETAKER   Why does it matter?

REGINA   I don't know…to leave.

CARETAKER   To leave, you just need to know where the exit is. Over there. I can take you. Certainly, for all the others, the thing is a bit…skirting…the regulations. I should report — or find out…. So, I don't know, maybe it would be better to wait until morning.

REGINA   *(looking high above)* The stars!

CARETAKER   They're the last ones. It'll soon be dawn.

REGINA   When did they bring me here?

CARETAKER   Not even a day has passed.

REGINA   Only? *(comes out with a small scream)* Ah…

CARETAKER   What is it?

REGINA   I just realized why this place isn't new to me. God… God…. I was here as a child. I was eleven years old, when my littlest sister died. She was with lots of others even littler than she was. In there.

REGINA *indicates the other doors. Without really realizing it, she moves a few steps as if to go there, to the children.*

CARETAKER   Don't go over there.

REGINA   Why?

CARETAKER   …You can't. And you would have to trample on the sleeping man. He didn't hear anything. See how fortunate he

Stormcloud

was. If I too had kept on sleeping now I wouldn't — what should I say — be responsible.

REGINA *(goes two more steps)* I won't trample on him.

CARETAKER Don't go. *(almost whispering)* There are too many.

REGINA Many?… *(with a scream)* And Milla is there! And the others, my little friends!

CARETAKER I don't know. Certainly.

REGINA *(She staggers. He supports her. She is quite shaken up.)* You were right. I shouldn't look. I want to leave now. Let me go, I beg you.

CARETAKER Of course. But not alone. I'll go with you. Then I'll come back. Where will you go? To your house, that's clear. But where is it? They'll be frightened.

REGINA No, at home I have no one.

CARETAKER No one? And elsewhere? A relative? A boyfriend?

REGINA Ah! I'll go to my boyfriend.

CARETAKER Oh, you have one. I'm glad.

REGINA I don't really know…

CARETAKER You don't know if you have a boyfriend?

REGINA This morning — you told me that it was this morning, so it must be true — two men told me that they wanted to marry me.

CARETAKER I see. You have to choose.

REGINA I want to go to the one who loves me more.

CARETAKER Who knows what he'll do, when he sees you.

REGINA They will both be beside themselves with joy. I'd like to know which one will be happier.

CARETAKER It's always something. *(indicates the* ATTENDANT*)* He sleeps. Sleeping, maybe he's among all the dead, and maybe the dead see the thoughts of the living. So right this minute he knows where you should go. You would need to ask him. But when he's able to answer you that'll mean he's come back, and then he won't remember and won't know what to tell us. You see how complicated it is.

REGINA Just go with me part of the way.

CARETAKER As you wish.

The CARETAKER *makes as if to leave.* REGINA *hesitates, perplexed, as if she is attracted to the tombs.*

REGINA *(under a spell)* And yet… *(but her whole body, with a jerk, rebels against her)* no, no, let's go.

REGINA *moves resolutely to the exit, and the* CARETAKER *follows with solemn respect.*

Stormcloud

Episode Three

Felice's room. Against the wall on the left, downstage, a bed. A small table in the middle of the room. The door is on the wall on the right. It is night. FELICE *stands in front of the table, preparing flowers in vases of various sizes and arranging them all around a portrait of Regina that is in the middle of the table.*

FELICE   There. *(He moves away to see the effect.)* A taller flower here…no, further back is better, *(moves the table further back)* so every time I enter, *(He goes back to the door on the right, opens it, exits halfway for an instant and reenters, looking immediately toward the table.)* there, on the spot, the precious image greets me. *(He turns to the table.)* And every day I will be here to place flowers before you, Regina. From now on my life is devoted to the memory of you. Over there, too, *(turning toward the bed)* I want you to be the first thing I see every morning, when I open my eyes and turn toward the light, like this.

FELICE *lays down on the bed and faces the wall, then like someone waking up, turns his glance toward the middle of the room to see the table.* FELICE *sees the door on the right open slowly, and* REGINA *appears at the threshold.*

FELICE   Who is it?… Ahhh… *(His voice is suffocated by fear.)* Noooo.… Go away.… What is it?… Go away.…

Half-thrown off the side of the bed, FELICE *backs away as far away as possible from the vision. His eyes are wide; his hands grope the blanket feverishly, as if to grab onto something.*

REGINA   It's me. I'm Regina. Not a day has passed, and you don't recognize me?

FELICE   *(faint)* No, it's not true. Regina is dead.

REGINA   She is reborn. I am arisen for you. Aren't you happy?

FELICE   It's not true. I don't believe it. It's not possible.… No one has ever.… *(He reels, with his arms in the air. Now he rises to his feet.)* Reborn, no one does that. Go away.…

REGINA   Felice, this isn't the kind of welcome I expected.

FELICE   I don't believe in miracles. I don't want to see them. Miracles frighten me.

Scene design for *Stormcloud*, Episode Three, by H. Blaetler. The Getty Research Institute, Los Angeles (910147).

Stormcloud

REGINA   It's not a miracle. Calm down. I wasn't dead, that's all. They were deceived, it seems.... I woke up a little bit ago, on top of a.... *(She shudders, and she doesn't dare complete the phrase.)* I was never dead.

FELICE   *(a little less frightened, but suspicious)* You weren't dead? They were deceived? *(takes a step toward her, stops himself, holds out his arms as if he is afraid she will come near)* I don't believe you. I can't comprehend it. It's something stronger than me. You say that you weren't dead? What does "dead" mean? No one knows, so one has to believe them, the others. You are on the list of the dead. They prayed for you. They lit candles. I saw you. I came to say goodbye to you, you know? You were beautiful, beautiful like that. *(He looks at the portrait and is enraptured.)* You see, I placed flowers for you, with my own hands. I'll put fresh ones there every morning. My life is here now, I'll spend it admiring you, from near and from afar. *(Not taking his eyes from the portrait, he moves away, toward the left.)*

REGINA   *(takes a step forward, reaches a hand toward the portrait, flattered)* My portrait.

FELICE   *(immediately)* Don't touch it. I won't allow it. No one may touch that image. It's something sacred, to be adored.

REGINA   And why don't you adore me?

FELICE   You are dead. Don't you see? That is not the portrait of a living person.

REGINA   Me.

FELICE   You want people to believe that you weren't dead? Not completely, perhaps. But you were in death, and if I.... *(Goes to step toward her, and he stops himself, frozen by an inexorable sense of horror.)* See? It would always be like this. Leave me alone. Let me live here *(He kneels before the portrait.)* in remembrance of you, like this, until the end of my days.

FELICE *has completed this last line without looking at* REGINA, *who exits.*

Massimo Bontempelli

Episode Four

The meadow from episode one. Advanced dawn. Throughout this episode, the sky brightens until it reaches, at the very end, the full luminosity of the beginning of the play. Onstage, MARZIO *is alone, thinking.*

MARZIO   *(after a pause, during which he looks around the sky and the meadow)* If everything lies within us, why look at things? If that which is living is in me, why have I come to seek, I think, the image of Regina? Because I need help from the plants, from that sky, from this wall where I saw her die? Oh, maybe Felice is right, and with him all the Felices on earth. It's the fault of our limited capacity. Everything that is in us overflows and becomes the world, and so we have to go toward the world, to reabsorb it into our soul to keep it nourished. *(pause)* Words: meanwhile, truth be told, deep down I ask myself just one question: "Where is Regina now?" No, to tell the truth, the real question I ask is this: "Where is my memory of Regina now?" *(He's getting agitated.)* I feel it appear and disappear in a strange restlessness in my brain, as if in a scene. I don't know how to seize it. I can't bring myself to immerse myself in the spirit world, where she is and has forgotten everything except herself, because maybe the Empyrean is this and nothing else. *(devastated)* I don't know anything. I can't do anything. Another hour like this and I'll envy Felice. *(Pause. He looks at the base of the wall, where Regina fell.)* She died here, like the children, therefore certainly she died of too much innocence. Here.

MARZIO *sits with his back against the wall, exactly at the point and in the posture in which he had found Regina. Then he leans his elbows on his knees and puts his head in his hands, covering his eyes. Pause.* REGINA *appears at the end of the street.*

REGINA   *(stops at the corner, calls softly)* Marzio.

MARZIO   I hear Regina's voice so clearly.

REGINA   It's me, Marzio.

MARZIO   The voice is clearer. If I answered her now, I think she would hear me. Regina!

REGINA   Why won't you look at me?

Stormcloud

MARZIO   Surely, now I could even see her. *(lifts his head, turns it and sees her)* Regina, it's you, really you...

MARZIO *gets up. They come toward each other, gushing. He takes her hand, draws her near to him, with immense affection.*

MARZIO   My darling.

REGINA   Marzio, aren't you afraid? Don't you think I'm a ghost? Aren't you amazed that I am not dead?

MARZIO   My true love, you are in my arms, I hear you, and I see you. All the rest was nothing. I don't need to know anymore.... I only know...only this. *(Gently,* REGINA *leans her head on his shoulders, and* MARZIO *kisses her on the head.)*

REGINA   *(standing on her tiptoes)* Are you happy?

MARZIO   I've come to know happiness. Happiness that will never change. Regina, come on, let's walk together. No, stay here, pressed against me. Darling, I don't know how to tell you how much I love you.

REGINA   I have never known you to be so simple, Marzio, and you frightened me a little. Why?

MARZIO   Why? Oh...I feel like I could tell you, but I don't know how to grasp a thought. I am all joy, only joy.... And I know it will always be this way, Regina, to the last faraway day. Come on. Let's hurry to plan our life, Regina.

REGINA   First I have an important confession to make.

MARZIO   No, nothing matters.

REGINA   Yes, I want to. Because it's horrible.

MARZIO   I don't believe it.

REGINA   Tonight I woke up *(with a shudder)* there, you understand me?

MARZIO   I don't know anything anymore.

REGINA   And when I realized I wasn't dead, I went outside and said to myself, "I must find...." But I didn't know yet, I didn't distinguish — this is the horrible thing — I didn't yet know that you were my love. And in that moment thinking of you I felt... before I told you I felt "fear," but that's not right, I wanted to

63

say "awe." That's it, to think of you, of my whole life with you, I felt intimidated. And, then, I was exhausted, dazed. I thought I was going toward something easier — I don't know how to say it — something simpler.... Oh, Marzio, before coming here I went to...to...

MARZIO   No, that's enough. Everything went fine. Let's think about what will be for us tomorrow.

REGINA   You know? A strange instinct brought me here to see you. Here where I said my last words to you. I didn't think consciously that you were here, no, and yet I couldn't do anything but come here. And coming, the children came to mind, and all that horrible grief when I saw them die, but now — this is horrendous, too — now I don't feel any more sadness. I think of them with peace. I think of them high up. I see them as angels of heaven, of a good heaven, where there is nothing to be afraid of.

MARZIO *and* REGINA *both look at the sky, which is now quite bright. And upstage they see five* CHILDREN *arrive, running and shouting with joy.*

REGINA   Look. *(perplexed at this sight and almost humbled)*

MARZIO   Let's go.

REGINA   Let me see them for a minute.

The five CHILDREN *approach, shouting among themselves.*

FIRST CHILD   We should play "Cops and Robbers."

SECOND CHILD   But that's better to play with more people.

THIRD CHILD   Come on.

FOURTH CHILD   I'll go home to call my brother.

THIRD CHILD   *(teasing)* Sure, an hour will pass before you go and come back.

FOURTH CHILD   I'm not a snail like you.

THIRD CHILD   Me, a snail? *(He throws himself at him.)*

FOURTH CHILD   Just a minute. *(He steps back, putting himself in position to fight.)*

FIFTH CHILD   Go, go!

FIRST CHILD   I bet on the snail.

Stormcloud

SECOND CHILD   But no, no. Fight later, or else what are we going to do?

FOURTH CHILD   (*backing into* REGINA) Oh....

FIFTH CHILD   (*to* REGINA) Ah, that's it. You play with us, too.

FIRST CHILD   Yes, I've seen you playing here lots of times.

FIVE CHILDREN   Yes, play, come on, then we'll be six — play!

SECOND CHILD   And him, too, (*indicates* MARZIO) makes seven.

MARZIO   But no, I don't know how to play.

FIVE CHILDREN   (*loudly*) Him too, you come, too. Yes, yes....

The CHILDREN *circle around and grab* MARZIO.

REGINA   (*taking charge*) Okay. He'll play, too, but now all of you in the middle.

FIVE CHILDREN   Okay. In the middle...we're ready...let's start.

REGINA   (*takes* MARZIO *by the hand*) Come.

MARZIO *barely lets* REGINA *pull him, but smiles in spite of himself.*

REGINA   Look, you know lots of things, but if you don't want to frighten me anymore, you have to learn one more thing. You have to learn to play.

REGINA *and* MARZIO *join the* CHILDREN, *who, shouting loudly, arrange themselves to begin the game.*

The End

Cinderella

A Show in Three Acts
(Five Episodes)

Massimo Bontempelli

A Note on the Text

I've translated from the only published version of the play: the 1942 *Cenerentola* (Rome: Edizioni della Cometa).

Upon invitation, Bontempelli wrote *Cinderella* for the Maggio Musicale Fiorentino festival, where it premiered to great fanfare in 1942 — being the centerpiece "prose" work to conclude the largely operatic festival — with Laura Adani in the title role and Anna Proclemer as the kind stepsister Antonia. Bontempelli won acclaim for the text itself and for the original music, while the work of director Corrado Pavolini and scenographer Gianni Vagnetti was judged by the theater magazine *Scenario* to be "rich with exquisite motifs." Luigi Fontanella has since commented upon the piece's highly original nature as, essentially, a "musical," an extremely rare phenomenon in Italian theater.[1] With performance in mind, I have made some adjustments to characters' names, which make them easier to pronounce within the English text. Lady Lark in the original is Donna Calandra (a "calandra" is a lark, though "Calandra" would also remind Italian readers of Bibbiena's *La Calandria* and of Calandrino, the gullible character in Giovanni Boccaccio's *Decameron*), Marina is Màrmara (a sea between the Aegean and the Bosphorus, which leads from Istanbul into the Black Sea). I have left Maestro Ademaro's name as-is, but often in the dialogue have simply changed references to him to "the maestro." Icarus is the Anglicization of Icaro (in Greek mythology, son of the craftsman Daedalus, who fell dead into the Aegean Sea). Màrmara and Icaro are just two of Bontempelli's many characters whose names derive from myth and/or from geographical regions or bodies of water. In Italian, Prince Charming is called "Il Principe Azzurro," literally, the Blue Prince, which, if nothing else, may be a nice indication for costume designers.

P.G.

---

1. See introduction, xlix n. 107.

Cinderella

Characters

CINDERELLA

LADY LARK, THE STEPMOTHER

MARINA, THE ELDER STEPSISTER

ANTONIA, THE OTHER STEPSISTER

THE FAIRY GODMOTHER

MAESTRO ADEMARO, THE HAIR STYLIST

ICARUS, A VIOLA PLAYER

PRINCE CHARMING

THE CHAMBERLAIN

COURTIERS

THE POLICE CAPTAIN

A FORTUNE-TELLER

LADIES AND GENTLEMEN

MUSICIANS

BUGLERS

TWO SCOUTS

FOUR STRETCHER-BEARERS

A HERALD

GUARDS

TWO HOMELY GIRLS

THEIR MAID

A PRETTY YOUNG GIRL

A COACHMAN

A GROUP OF BOYS

THE PEOPLE

Massimo Bontempelli

ACT ONE

Episode One

A terrace on the roof of Cinderella's house. CINDERELLA *(in a large apron and heavy clogs) and the* FAIRY GODMOTHER *(dressed like a peasant woman, with a handkerchief on her head) look at the sky.*

CINDERELLA One, two. Already two stars.

GODMOTHER There's another breaking through over there. You can barely see it. Look. Now it's bright.

CINDERELLA I see it. That makes three. And four. Five.

GODMOTHER Any minute now the sky all around them will be dark.

CINDERELLA Another one, two more. Oh! They're too fast.

GODMOTHER I think that in the beginning the sky was empty, black without stars.

CINDERELLA Wasn't it really scary?

GODMOTHER Of course. Then the first ones that they sent — over there, maybe, or there, on the edges all around — had to twinkle all on their own, in that cold space. They were just barely visible, and very, very pale.

CINDERELLA They were ashamed.

GODMOTHER Exactly, and they tried to hide below the horizon.

CINDERELLA Look how many have come, from all over! They're like sheep. Who can keep count now?

GODMOTHER You see how even everything on the ground is set to look at the sky.

CINDERELLA You can hardly see anything down there anymore.

GODMOTHER But you hear it. If you listen hard, you hear it.

They lean toward the countryside, listening.

CHORUS OF THE EARTH

> Life, another day
> extinguished, another night
> comes to light.
> One by one the stars come.

One missing still.
That star
forever will be missing,
until the last of nights.
When that star appears
alone in the sky it will dwell.
The entire sky will be that single star.

Silence.

CINDERELLA It's over. It was lovely.

GODMOTHER But do you still hear it?

The harmony of the chorus continues softly, almost like slow breathing.

CINDERELLA *(listening)* Now you can only hear breathing. It's strange how the entire earth breathes as one.

GODMOTHER At night, all things become sisters.

CINDERELLA You can no longer tell the sound of the water from the sound of the leaves.

GODMOTHER Everything becomes one again, like at the beginning of the world.

CINDERELLA *(listening and almost singing along)* All one, all one....

All at once, the lively sound of sleigh bells approaching, while the chorus stops.

GODMOTHER It's the maestro's carriage.

CINDERELLA Too bad.

GODMOTHER You have to go help your stepmother and sisters dress for Prince Charming's party.

The sleigh bells stop.

CINDERELLA He's here.

GODMOTHER Let's go.

CINDERELLA *and the* FAIRY GODMOTHER *begin to exit through a trapdoor in the floor of the terrace. The* CHORUS *begins again.*

CINDERELLA *(stops a moment and listens)* Again? But as soon as they leave, let's come back to listen to the earth sleep.

GODMOTHER Yes, the night loves you.

Massimo Bontempelli

CINDERELLA *and the* FAIRY GODMOTHER *descend and disappear. The* CHORUS OF THE EARTH *gets louder and then begins to fade again. It stops the moment the new episode begins.*

Episode Two

A vast dressing room in Cinderella's house. A tall three-piece mirror in the upstage left corner. Part of the sky can be seen through a window in the upstage wall. A table along the stage-left wall. A clothes-rack.

Onstage, CINDERELLA, *the* FAIRY GODMOTHER, *the stepmother* (LADY LARK), *the two stepsisters* (MARINA *and* ANTONIA) *and* MAESTRO ADEMARO. MARINA *and* ANTONIA, *in dressing gowns, on two seats side by side, center stage facing the public* (MARINA *stage right,* ANTONIA *stage left*), *each holding a mirror. Behind them, standing, is* MAESTRO ADEMARO *with curling iron in one hand and comb in the other. He uses the iron on one, the comb on the other, alternating between the two sisters.*

CINDERELLA *stands at his side and serves him diligently. From a stand full of implements a bit further back on the right, she takes a hairpin, then a tin etc., according to the* MAESTRO*'s indications. She holds a little spirit stove in one hand, on which he warms the iron every so often, and in the other a tray in which he places the comb.*

LADY LARK *is already all made up, combed, and dressed for the ball. She sits rigidly on a stool, towards stage left, with her hands tense, her neck still, careful to let everything set without ruining her make-up, hair or dress.*

On the right in the corner, in front of a little table, the FAIRY GODMOTHER, *with her back to the house, plays solitaire. Seen this way, she seems like a lifeless old woman. Occasionally she murmurs.*

As he works, the MAESTRO *chatters nonstop.*

MAESTRO   *(frenetic)* This curl curlier, *(touches* MARINA *with the iron)* this one a bit more ecstatic, *(touches* ANTONIA *with the comb)* classic beauty on the left, (*to* ANTONIA) capricious pleasantness on the right, (*to* MARINA) here the metaphysical, there the picturesque, there a vortex, here a stairway to heaven. Then all the rest in sparse and logical order, contained and explosive *(indicating various curls on each head)*: helix hook funnel snail tube sliver dart; curls as backdrop and curls of atmosphere, ellipsoids and parabolas — please girly, (*to* CINDERELLA) a number-four hairpin, thank you — thus from my very hands are born Marina the perennial blond and Antonia the brunette undaunted, while the mother is already done and drying, (*indicates* LADY LARK) splayed like a lizard on a wall — you can put this back now *(giving* CINDERELLA *the irons)* — one, two, three. And if we could see through walls, that one and that there, the entire city is a vast field where the heads I've prepared for Prince Charming's party are blooming, an organ keyboard on which I composed and played prelude, fugue and chorale, all all all of them done by me, heads of every hue, outside I mean and inside done by no one because there's no need — thanks girly *(to* CINDERELLA, *who offers him a towel)* — what we perceive is the life and substance of things — one second with scissor number three (*to* CINDERELLA) — appearances: women, thought, flowers, things, works and days, and the air, and the stars. *(He draws near the upstage window, drying his hands.)* Those stars, tresses of the night sky awakened: they're arriving from the far away Antipodes. They're still sleepy, none of them wants to be first, then they come crashing down all at once. The sky lifts its head from twilight pillows and shakes it. So when within an hour you are dancing, I Maestro Ademaro will be doing the hair of the sky. And when between one dance and another the partner with his arm around your waist takes you to the terrace to look at the sky — because there is no ball without a terrace and there is no partner without an arm wrapped around — then you will think for a second of the maestro who brushes Andromeda's mane, refreshes Cassiopeia's waves, curls Orsa Major's tail and the eyebrows of Orsa Minor, plants the Arctic Crown like a diadem. *(He's come back behind his patients.[2])* Girly, *(to* CINDERELLA) a gilt star for here *(She gives him one.)* — no, two. *(She gives him another. He puts it in* MARINA'*s hair.)* And two white petals for here. *(She gives him two gardenias. He puts them on* ANTONIA'*s head but immediately reconsiders and takes them off.)* No, here nothing.

---

2. The use of the word "patients" here might seem odd, as the Maestro is characterized as an artist, not a doctor. And yet, in the context of Bontempelli's oeuvre, it is not so strange. He had a tendency to mix his metaphors, blurring lines so that his artisans and professionals — be they tailors, doctors, innkeepers — often resemble artists and therefore sometimes magicians. This is in keeping with the principles of Novecento, discussed in the introduction, pp. xxv–xxvi.

ANTONIA   Because I am classical beauty.

LADY LARK   *(still on her stool, speaks, moving her mouth as little as possible)* Maestro, I think I am dry.

MAESTRO   Your grace may move, but don't talk too much, not least because it's not necessary, given that, twice widowed, you no longer have a husband to sweep away or submerge.

LADY LARK *gets up and takes a few cautious steps. She goes to look at herself in the tall mirror.*

MARINA   *(looking in the hand mirror, very respectfully)* Maestro, don't you think a third star here would fill this little gap?

MAESTRO   Not all gaps are to be filled, young lady. Please, girly, *(to* CINDERELLA*)* the second mirror for the indirect view.

CINDERELLA *takes two mirrors from the stand and goes to place them before the two sisters — with her back to the public — holding the mirrors tightly before each one.*

MARINA   At more of an angle, you fool.

ANTONIA   *(after looking at herself, dismisses* CINDERELLA *with an imperial wave)* Fine, thank you, sister.

MARINA   *(furiously, to* ANTONIA*)* I don't want you calling her "sister." I'm your sister — everyone sees it at a glance — not that groundhog.

ANTONIA   No one sees it. The other day someone asked if you were my grandmother.

MARINA   *(yells)* That's not true! You're saying that because you're jealous. (*She jumps up, as if advancing toward* ANTONIA.)

ANTONIA   *(Frightened, she gets up and takes a step backward.)* Don't touch me!

MAESTRO   *(who has been keeping a watchful eye on them during the squabble)* Stop! *(They stop instantly.)* The conclusion of this first-rate row is to be postponed until after the ball, for the obvious reason of respect for my work.

LADY LARK   He's right. Please pardon them, maestro. *(to* CINDERELLA, *who at that moment passes by her)* It's all your fault. *(She's about to strike her, but* CINDERELLA *steps sweetly aside and at the same time* LADY LARK *realizes that with the brusque movement she has messed up a puff on her sleeve.)*

Cinderella

MARINA *and* ANTONIA *go to look at themselves in the full-length mirror.*

MAESTRO *(from a distance)* You are perfect, in every movement of the head, which from the top down generates a person's every motion. Perfect, in tranquility and in tumult. Goodbye.

LADY LARK   Thank you, maestro. Girls, do your duty.

MARINA and ANTONIA   *(together)* Thank you. Thank you. *(They go to him at the door, and with a bow, kiss his hand, then back away.)*

MAESTRO   *(at the door, to* LADY LARK, *solemnly and contritely)* To thank me properly one would have to find words of prayer. As every morning you thank the Supreme Entity that gave you life, so you should thank me, who, doing your hair, gives this life its purpose and means of expression. *(again relaxed)* Goodbye then to Marina and Antonia recreated by me, to their mother who in her time went through the pain of preparing them for me, and also to my modest helper, and to the godmother who was a fairy and is no longer, because all men and women have realized they are fairies and magicians. The history of the world is a fable, and the rest doesn't count. Until another party. *(exits)*

MARINA *and* ANTONIA *remain gazing in ecstasy at the door through which the* MAESTRO *has exited. The music of the sleigh bells starts close by and instantly fades away.* CINDERELLA *puts the stand in a corner, places all the objects that were on it into a cupboard and straightens the chairs.*

LADY LARK   Hurry up. What are you doing? It's getting late.

MARINA   *(to* CINDERELLA*)* You, the dress. What are you waiting for? *(Meanwhile, humming, she practices a dance step.)*

CINDERELLA *takes a dress from the clothes-rack and goes to put in on* MARINA, *over her head, very carefully.*

MARINA   Slowly, fool. The hair.

LADY LARK   Remember, girls, that I don't want to dance. Not at all. When they start to approach me, "Lady Lark, a turn with me, one with me..." and they insist, you need to say, "It's true, mama never dances. She made a vow." Because I know how they are, one turn, another turn, and pretty soon they are losing their heads. But I want to be left in peace, and I don't like to see them suffer.

Massimo Bontempelli

CINDERELLA *backs up two steps to look at* MARINA *and goes back to her, kneels down to flatten a wrinkle in her skirt.*

ANTONIA   *(like she is acting)* "Certainly." "I beg you." "I wouldn't have expected this from a gentleman."

MARINA   Are you crazy?

LADY LARK   What's wrong with you?

ANTONIA   I'm practicing saying a few words with classic dignity. "Dear Prince, I've just come back from the terrace, where I was admiring the sky."

LADY LARK   I'm always the first to be ready.

CINDERELLA *has come to help* ANTONIA *get into her dress. Meanwhile* MARINA *practices a difficult step.*

MARINA   I don't understand. This morning I could do the *piquè* wonderfully…ah, yes, delightful. Let's hope they don't dance the conga. No one is ever enough in the know. But my forte has always been the arabesque.

ANTONIA   You didn't mess up my hair, did you?

CINDERELLA *circles* ANTONIA, *fixes a curl on her neck, and backs away. Throughout these silent operations* CINDERELLA *appears attentive and calm.*

ANTONIA   Thank you, sister.

MARINA   I told you to stop it!

LADY LARK   Finally. Let's go.

ANTONIA, MARINA *and* LADY LARK, *in that order, leave without remembering to say goodbye to* CINDERELLA *or to the* FAIRY GODMOTHER. *They speak as they leave, heads held high, without turning around.*

ANTONIA   I'm sure to be the prettiest. *(arrives at the exit)*

MARINA   *(reaches her through dance steps)* I think this time the prince will lose his head over me. *(The two of them leave.)*

LADY LARK   It seems to me that in my day we weren't so stupid. *(She exits.)*

CINDERELLA *and the* FAIRY GODMOTHER *remain on stage.* CINDERELLA *stares at the door where her stepmother and sisters have exited. At*

Cinderella

their exit, the smile disappears from her face, which instantly becomes pained. She backs up as far as the table and then she turns, falling into the chair, and with her head in her hands throws herself on the table and dissolves into a puddle of tears.

GODMOTHER *(jumps up and comes to* CINDERELLA'S *side)* What's the matter, Cinderella?

CINDERELLA *(without lifting her head, between sobs)* You know, godmother.

GODMOTHER No.

CINDERELLA *(lifting her tear-covered face)* I want to go to the prince's ball.

GODMOTHER To the ball?

CINDERELLA Yes.

GODMOTHER You?

CINDERELLA Yes.

GODMOTHER Like Marina and Antonia?

CINDERELLA Yes.

GODMOTHER *(still incredulous)* Really?

CINDERELLA So much. *(She gets up and just stands there, disconsolate.)*

GODMOTHER But you know that it's a foolish desire.

CINDERELLA I know.

GODMOTHER *(putting an arm around her, walks her a few steps around the room)* We were so happy, the two of us, the other evenings…when they go to bed and our time begins, Cinderella. You liked it when I explained so many things about the world: the sea, the plants, the light. When I showed you the night sky. *(She pushes her gently toward the upstage window.)* Look. All the constellations are out. The people sent up from the earth: warriors, hunters, poets, emperors, dogs, families. Are you listening to me?

CINDERELLA Yes, godmother, but you've already told me.

GODMOTHER That's true. How happy you were when you were able to find the Big Dipper. In the beginning you could never find the handle. Look at it. Now it's right in the middle.

CINDERELLA   I see it. It's beautiful.

GODMOTHER   Everything in the sky is beautiful. *(They turn back towards center.)* And the entire sea. And at the very peaks of the highest mountains, with multicolored snow. On the ground below there are many beautiful things, and some that are ugly. And inside each of us — oh no, inside of us everything is beautiful, too.

CINDERELLA   I don't think so, godmother.

GODMOTHER   *(resolute)* Yes. What is born in us is all beautiful and all good. If it is ugly it's when it gets mixed with something that comes from outside. You have never been like you are tonight, Cinderella. Do you know what this is called? It's called "sadness." Tonight you are sad.

CINDERELLA   *(hanging her head)* You know that I don't understand.

GODMOTHER   I know. All the other times when your stepmother and sisters went to bed, or for a ride, I never taught you anything but good things.

CINDERELLA   *(with an immense sigh)* But tonight they didn't go to sleep, they didn't go for a ride, they went *(with hardly a voice)* to Prince Charming's ball.

GODMOTHER   *(pained)* This is how sadness is born.

CINDERELLA   But why didn't they take me, too? *(bitterly)* Oh, godmother, why aren't you a fairy anymore?

GODMOTHER   Who said so? Why do you ask me that?

CINDERELLA   *(with more obstinate anguish)* Why aren't you a fairy anymore?

GODMOTHER   Oh, that hairdresser, the maestro, he almost got it. People were too foolish. God didn't make the sun for a city of moles, dug out in the floor of a cellar. In the beginning, when I was just realizing I was a fairy, what joy! I dreamed that I could do good, answer all kinds of prayers. It's crazy to think back on it. From me, because I was a fairy, girls wanted to know if their boyfriends betrayed them with the maid. Old ladies wanted to know if the cat who was missing for three days would come back. Young or old, if I offer to send them from here to the Milky Way with a spell, the first thing they ask is if they need to

Cinderella

dress for evening or for travel. Men worse than women. More than anything *they* asked me which stocks to invest in. Enough. Enough. Enough with magic. Magic? You plant a seed in the earth and in the March sun, green sprouts, a flower comes up and becomes fruit, with a bunch of other seeds, and then the snow comes to shelter it until the new spring. *That* is the miracle. Sea water evaporates and travels across the sky, and the mountain makes a river that returns to the sea, and meanwhile plants and animals drink and bathe in the ever-fresh current. Fairy? To be a fairy, you just have to know you are one. Every woman and every man is fairy and magician, but they don't know it. And this, the not-knowing, is their gravest fault. The greatest magic is intelligence, from which goodness is born. That is the spell for being happy. But, instead, today you are sad.

CINDERELLA Yes.

GODMOTHER If you are sad, you'll become mean.

CINDERELLA The sisters are always mean.

GODMOTHER They're mean because they are unhappy.

CINDERELLA Why are they unhappy?

GODMOTHER Because they don't understand.

CINDERELLA But as we speak, they are arriving at the prince's ball, and they are happy.

GODMOTHER No, no.

CINDERELLA Oh, godmother. Why aren't you a fairy anymore, but really?

GODMOTHER *(a little worked up)* Why are you asking me this? Who says? Do you want me to prove it to you? Why do you keep asking me this?

CINDERELLA *(looking at the floor)* If you are a fairy, you need to make it so that the sisters don't get to the ball.

GODMOTHER *(she lifts* CINDERELLA's *head and looks into her eyes)* Look how the sadness has already become meanness and envy. *(irritated)* No.

CINDERELLA So then it's true that you're no longer a fairy, seriously.

GODMOTHER Even talking like that, you are mean.

CINDERELLA I have nothing left in the sky or on earth. *(She throws herself down on the table again with head in hands, sobbing desperately.)*

GODMOTHER Cinderella, Cinderella, Cinderella, I don't want you to suffer. I'll do anything so you won't suffer. Anything, yes, even this: I'll be a fairy again, one time, for you, so you won't cry. To spare you. Look at me.

CINDERELLA *(lifts her head, almost frightened)* What do you mean?

GODMOTHER It means, what you want most will be done, and done right away.

CINDERELLA *(frightened)* What I wanted? What I said? Then —

GODMOTHER I'll send you to the ball. In ten minutes you'll be at that ball. Instantly, if you wish.

CINDERELLA No, no —

GODMOTHER *(disappointed)* You don't want to go to Prince Charming's ball anymore?

CINDERELLA *(right away)* Oh, yes.... But how?

GODMOTHER Don't worry about that. Believe in me.

CINDERELLA I believe, I believe, but.... *(suddenly she looks at herself)* Dressed like this? No, then. No.

GODMOTHER *(laughs)* Don't be afraid. I know. I know that fairy magic has to begin with the dress. For me, too. Do you think I could stay like this, like when I play solitaire *(indicating the cards still sitting on the table)* while the sisters fight? You don't believe in me anymore, and goodbye magic. Watch. *(She rises, that is, she gets taller. With both hands she takes the handkerchief from her head and swats at the tangle of hair that was covering her forehead, which appears white and sleek, and her face is luminous. She wiggles, and her dress becomes long and sparkling.)*

CINDERELLA Godmother, how beautiful you are. *(clasps her hands tightly)* I've never seen you like this.

GODMOTHER Now we'll take care of you. *(She caresses* CINDERELLA*'s forehead and hair, which comes loose and falls to her shoulders. She gently takes her face in her hands and breathes lightly on her forehead. She moves away, and* CINDERELLA*'s face becomes luminous*

Cinderella

and ecstatic. *She goes back to her and waves her hands from top to bottom of the apron, which falls away as if transformed into a long striped skirt, pearl-colored, it too illuminated.)* Look at you. I work faster than the Maestro.

CINDERELLA *(For a moment remains transfixed and very shy, then goes slowly toward the tall mirror; after another silence she claps her hands with joy.)* Is it me? Is it me? *(She jumps, with a big noise from her clogs. Mortified, she looks at her feet.)* Ohh....

GODMOTHER What is it? It's true. I forgot something important. Wait *(looks around)*, what can we use, with a system of purest magic, to make two slippers?

CINDERELLA *(looks around herself, very anxious, with hardly a voice)* God....

GODMOTHER Ah — ha! *(goes to look at the cards on the table)* Let's take the shoes of a queen. *(chooses)* The Queen of Diamonds is the most elegant. *(with one hand she takes the card, with the other she smoothes it, like magicians do, as if to take something out)* You just have to make it bigger. *(She looks at the little feet of* CINDERELLA, *who in her impatience has taken off her clogs.)* Look, ladies and gentlemen, a beautiful little satin slipper, *(meanwhile she has repeated the motion and extracted the second)* and here is its companion.

CINDERELLA *(who has followed the operation with wonder, every moment increasingly lit up with joy, claps her hands and jumps up and down shouting)* Bravo!

GODMOTHER Violà! Take them. One, two. *(She throws them to her across the room.)*

CINDERELLA *(grabbing them and putting them on)* Okay, Okay, I'm ready. Now what?

GODMOTHER There's nothing left but to go. To find, as they say, the means of transport. There's the classic system of the pumpkin turned carriage, with rats and mice as horses and coachmen, but where to find the mice in this disinfected world? Certainly there's a more modern system. *(She looks around as if to orient herself.)* Tell me, where exactly is Prince Charming's palace?

CINDERELLA *(right away)* Over there, godmother. *(indicates toward the upstage wall)* Wait. *(still indicating, more certain as she continues to talk)* First, there's the field, then you go down to skirt around a ditch that turns like this, but then it turns straight and opens right out onto the main road. At the end of the road there's a long embankment that goes right to where the palace gardens begin. That's it, in exactly that direction. *(Again she indicates upstage.)*

GODMOTHER   Good. I was saying, there's an easier way. It exploits the elasticity of space.

CINDERELLA   *(wide-eyed)* What?

GODMOTHER   Put yourself like this. *(She stands her up straight with her face to the upstage wall.)* I will contract space until this wall touches the palace wall. It will open, and you'll find yourself in the courtyard. Climb the big staircase. You'll hear the music. Follow it, and go in.

CINDERELLA   God!

GODMOTHER   No, if you don't have the courage, don't go.

CINDERELLA   I have the courage, I have the courage. It can be done?

GODMOTHER   *(solemn)* But first, listen very carefully. This power lasts only until midnight. Take great care. If the clock finishes striking midnight and you are not yet outside, on the road, alone, farewell to all! The spell is over. You go back to being as you were before, dressed as before —

CINDERELLA   In the apron?

GODMOTHER   In the apron, yes, and your messy hair, and far, far away from here, and so how will you return, on foot, at night —

CINDERELLA   In clogs. No, no, I'll leave on time.

GODMOTHER   Before the last stroke of midnight.

CINDERELLA   Before the last stroke of midnight.

The GODMOTHER *silently kisses* CINDERELLA *on the top of her head, then puts her back in place and lifts her hands toward the wall. The whole stage goes dark. Gradually the walls light up again, as music begins to be heard: first far away, then little by little it gets closer. When the music is very close and the wall intensely illuminated, the scene goes black again.*

End of Act One

Cinderella

ACT TWO

Episode Three

The ballroom. Dazzling light. GENTLEMEN *and* LADIES *seated along the walls, among them* MARINA *and* LADY LARK. *A few couples dance.* ANTONIA *dances with* PRINCE CHARMING. *In the corner on the right of the proscenium begins (and evidently continues inside) the group of musicians, among them* ICARUS. *Against a wall, a table with flowers and fruit.*

Through the open doors dinner guests can be seen mingling in other rooms.

From the people, both from those dancing and from the others, comes the hum of conversation, from which can be picked out: "Prince," "Always always," "Charming," "so loving," "destiny"....

After maybe thirty seconds (at a moment in which the music plays lightly in the background), a soft knock on the upstage door, which then opens.

CINDERELLA *appears in the doorway, where three steps descend into the room. She stops, dazzled, on the top step.*

GENTLEMAN *(who was sitting and suddenly stands)* Who is this damsel?

MANY *(From various places they look and, in admiration, rise to their feet.)* Who is she? Who is she? Who is she?

The dancing couples turn toward the door and separate. Among the musicians the FIRST VIOLIN *sees* CINDERELLA, *rises and stops playing. The rest of his companions similarly rise. All of the doorways fill with people come to admire. Various voices. (This has all happened very quickly.)*

PRINCE *(enraptured, leaves* ANTONIA *in the middle of the room and goes attentively toward* CINDERELLA*)* Mademoiselle, you are most welcome. *(He offers her his right arm.)*

CINDERELLA *(gives him her hand and timidly, step by step, descends)* Thank you.

PRINCE Why is you voice trembling?

CINDERELLA I don't know. It's natural.

Prince Charming's ball, Act Two, in the 1942 Maggio Musicale Fiorentino debut production of *Cinderella*, directed by Corrado Pavolini. Scenario 11.6 (June 1942): 205. Courtesy of the Biblioteca Nazionale, Roma.

PRINCE It's not natural. We are the ones who should tremble, seeing you materialize here.

CINDERELLA One trembles when she is afraid.

PRINCE One trembles in front of an angel, too.

VARIOUS COURTIERS What a response! What a lovely answer! Our prince knows just what to say.

PRINCE What is your name?

CINDERELLA Me? My name... that is, they call me, at home.... *(Looking up, she meets the glances of the* SISTERS *and* STEPMOTHER, *who fail to recognize her.)* They call me whatever you would like, Sir Prince Charming.

MANY *(applauding enthusiastically)* Exquisite. Sweet. Profound.

PRINCE But I already told you: an angel. That's it. I will call you Celestial Angel.

CINDERELLA *(with reverence)* Alright.

GENERAL MURMUR Celestial.... Angel...Angel...Angel from heaven.

PRINCE Do you come from afar?

CINDERELLA *(embarrassed)* I come from *(indicating in any direction)* — over there.

EVERYONE Ohhh. *(They turn and look in that direction.)*

PRINCE But, that place, wherever you are from, what do you call it, precisely?

CINDERELLA *(after a bit of hesitation)* Maybe I can't tell you, prince.

A FEW ENTHUSIASTS It's obvious: from heaven. Of course, from heaven...heaven...heaven....

PRINCE Naturally. From heaven. Permit me to take a turn around the floor with you. That way everyone can see you close-up.

The PRINCE *takes* CINDERELLA *by the hand and walks her slowly around the room, stopping in front of some* PEOPLE, *who will be indicated. Each rises as they pass, showing reverence.*

PRINCE This is a court minister.

CINDERELLA How can he be a minister without a beard?

MINISTER *(smiling)* It's a question of practicality.

PRINCE *(severely)* Do you understand, excellency? You will let your beard grow. *(They pass.)* These are my dignitaries. And this is the chamberlain.

CHAMBERLAIN *(bowing)* At your service, mademoiselle.

CINDERELLA What is a chamberlain?

CHAMBERLAIN The highest of the dignitaries.

CINDERELLA But what does he do?

CHAMBERLAIN The most difficult things. Will you allow me? This is my wife, lady of the court, and this is my daughter, court damsel. *(reverence)*

CINDERELLA What a strange family. *(They pass.)*

PRINCE Here is the police captain. And this is my fortune-teller.

CINDERELLA Oh! What fortunes do you tell? Of the past or the future?

FORTUNE-TELLER The present.

PRINCE And here is the beautiful Antonia, with whom I was dancing when you appeared.

CINDERELLA She really is very beautiful.

MARINA And I'm her sister.

CINDERELLA You see it right away. And this *(indicating the* STEPMOTHER*)* is a third sister? *(Someone laughs. mortified)* Did I say something wrong?

LADY LARK Nothing. They are laughing because I am their mother, Lady Lark.

CINDERELLA Really? *(They arrive at the orchestra.)* Oh, introduce me to them.

PRINCE But they are the musicians. *(He'd move away from them.)*

CINDERELLA But they are dressed so nicely. *(To the* FIRST VIOLIN, *touching his instrument.)* Do you mind if I touch it?

FIRST VIOLIN *(offering it, enthusiastically)* No, in fact, please, princess.

CINDERELLA *(confused by the title)* But I'm not *(plucking a string)* oh....

Cinderella

ALL THE MUSICIANS *(coming forward, each offering his instrument)* Please.... Mine, too.... This one, princess.... Thanks.... Thank you....

CINDERELLA *(has plucked two or three violins, sees* ICARUS, *who has a viola, but doesn't offer it)* This one, too?

ICARUS *(quickly pulling the viola away)* No, it will go out of tune.

CINDERELLA Oh, goodness, have I offended you? *(indicating the viola)* But why is it a little bit bigger than the others?

ICARUS Because it's a viola.

CINDERELLA Viola? *(suddenly with a lunge she plucks at a number of violins with both hands, then claps her hands joyfully)* Goodness, a ball is so much fun!

PRINCE But if no one dances, it's no longer a ball. *(to the* CHAMBERLAIN*)* Time to dance.

CHAMBERLAIN *(to the room)* It's time to dance.

Numerous couples get in position to dance. The music starts, and the PRINCE *and* CINDERELLA *dance, the other couples behind them. As before, from the confused hum emerge certain words: "angel," "from the sea," "extraordinary," "even more," "his highness."... After two turns the* PRINCE *and* CINDERELLA *stop, and everyone stops. The two of them are at the forestage.*

PRINCE You are light as...as...

CINDERELLA A feather?

PRINCE That's it, a feather. An angel feather.

CINDERELLA I think that a little bird's feather would be lighter than the feather of an angel, which is really big.

PRINCE You must excuse me if this party isn't as nice as those you've certainly been to where you are from.

CINDERELLA Who said that I come from somewhere else?

PRINCE Everyone would've recognized you if you were from here.

CINDERELLA Why have they stopped dancing?

PRINCE Because I stopped, and I'm the prince.

CINDERELLA And why did you stop?

PRINCE Because…because balls are not made only for dancing.

CINDERELLA Really? And what else are they made for?

PRINCE For many other things.

CINDERELLA Tell me one.

PRINCE I'll tell you two.

CINDERELLA Thank you.

PRINCE First, they are made for — besides dancing — arranging engagements.

CINDERELLA *(clapping her hands)* How wonderful. How many engagements happen at one party?

PRINCE According to… *(looking around)* there are about fifty girls and young men here…. *(calling)* Chamberlain.

CHAMBERLAIN Here I am, highness.

PRINCE How many engagements are arranged per party?

CHAMBERLAIN According to the Office of Statistics, the average is about 19 percent. Tonight there should be nine and one half engagements.

CINDERELLA Oh, the poor guy who's the half! What will he do?

CHAMBERLAIN We'll fix it with another party.

CINDERELLA But that's too few.

PRINCE And how many should there be?

CINDERELLA Everybody.

PRINCE Alright. *(to the* CHAMBERLAIN*)* Give the order that before the end of the ball everyone will be engaged.

CINDERELLA *(entreats him)* The half, too. *(to the* PRINCE*)* But, like this — because it's an order — I don't like that.

PRINCE Then, chamberlain, suspend the order.

CINDERELLA God, you can't say a word.

PRINCE Your every wish is my command.

CINDERELLA I don't like commands.

PRINCE What do you like?

CINDERELLA Dancing, and to see dancing.

PRINCE *(looks around)* But why is no one dancing?

CINDERELLA Now I know. Because the two of us are not dancing.

PRINCE *(impassioned)* Thank you.

CINDERELLA *(shocked)* For what?

PRINCE *(pathetic)* For saying "the two of us."

CINDERELLA I don't understand.

PRINCE *(looking at the crowd again)* Dance.

CHAMBERLAIN *(to the crowd)* Dance.

Many begin to dance again, but tentatively. Even the music is played softly.

PRINCE *(putting his arms around her to dance)* And us? "The two of us?"

CINDERELLA Just a minute. And the second?

PRINCE What second?

CINDERELLA You said that the parties are also used for other things, and you started, "First, for engagements." And "second"?

PRINCE What a memory you have. Too much of one, for a damsel.

CINDERELLA And you too little, for a prince. So, the second?

PRINCE For scheming. Over there, *(indicates the door in back on the left)* the engagement terrace. Over there, *(indicates the door down front on the left)* the situation room.

CINDERELLA What is scheming?

PRINCE My God, for example, when someone wants an appointment....

CINDERELLA What's an appointment?

PRINCE An appointment?... These things one learns little by little.

CINDERELLA How I'd like to watch.

PRINCE Engagements or scheming?

CINDERELLA Both.

PRINCE But first?

CINDERELLA First the engagements.

PRINCE That's the easiest. See those two (*pointing to a* COUPLE) dancing with their heads so close together? That's the beginning.

CINDERELLA It's lovely. And then?

PRINCE Look at those others, there. When they dance, they stop a moment, like that, to look at each other better, then they start again without saying another word....

CINDERELLA And they look like little puppy-dogs.

PRINCE Yes, then they are already quite advanced. In fact, look, look. They're going behind the column. Now they're not dancing any more. They think no one sees them — that's important, thinking that no one sees — and slowly, slowly they go. There, (*the* COUPLE *exits onto the terrace*) the engagement is almost done.

A break in the dancing. People move toward the upstage exit, speaking sottovoce.

CINDERELLA But where are they going?

PRINCE On the terrace. There you lean on the parapet and look at the stars.

CINDERELLA Oh, like the maestro said.

PRINCE There are certainly at least five or six couples on the terrace looking at the stars.

CINDERELLA Should we go watch?

PRINCE Gladly. (*offering his arm*) But (*stops*) you know, to go in two onto the terrace you have to have begun the engagement a little. It's prescribed. Would you like us to get engaged?

CINDERELLA For how long?

PRINCE What do you mean for how long? Until we get married. As soon as possible. Are you happy?

CINDERELLA (*Frightened, she backs away.*) No, no.

PRINCE (*floored*) Why "no, no"? What strange behavior.

CINDERELLA (*mortified*) I'm not familiar with these things, I'm sorry. They are new customs.

PRINCE *(laughing)* They are very old customs. But don't you realize any other girl I would have made this proposal to would've fainted with joy?

CINDERELLA *(laughing)* I don't know how to faint.

PRINCE But you weren't even happy.

CINDERELLA Yes, sir prince, I am happy.

PRINCE Well? Then don't call me "sir prince" anymore. And you, what should I call you? Ah, it's been determined: "Angel." Yes, Celestial Angel, do you think I was kidding? No, no. I love you already. I truly love you. I want you to be my bride. I want to make you princess, then queen....

CINDERELLA *(terrified)* No, no. Such things aren't for me.

PRINCE Oh, really, I don't understand you.

CINDERELLA *(distressed)* It's...before I was having fun, but not anymore.

PRINCE That's fine. My words are a serious thing. I'm not saying them for the sake of enjoyment.

CINDERELLA *(clapping her hands)* Good, okay. First I want to have fun and dance a little more, no? Then we can talk about it again.

PRINCE What a strange creature. You really want to drive me mad. Each word you say to me should anger me, drive me away, but instead what you say exhilarates me, Celestial Angel, Celestial Angel, dear....

CINDERELLA Oh, now, don't feel bad.

CHAMBERLAIN *(approaching with reverence)* Highness, her majesty the queen mother awaits you in the throne room for her goodnight kiss on the forehead.

PRINCE I'm ready, chamberlain; I leave this miraculous guest in your care. Make sure her every desire is satisfied. *(to* CINDERELLA*)* He will represent me among you for a few minutes. It's a privilege of his appointment.

CINDERELLA Oh then, *(pointing at the* CHAMBERLAIN*)* that's what an appointment is.

PRINCE   Until later. But first, *(going to the table where there is a basket of candied fruit)* I am certain that you will like the candied oranges *(gives them to her)* and these fresh mandarins *(gives them to her).*

CINDERELLA   *(taking the fruit with both hands)* Thank you, sir prince.

PRINCE   Permit me. *(He hurries away, turns a moment to look at her, and exits through the door in back on the left.)*

TWO COURTIERS *cautiously appear at the downstage left door.*

CHAMBERLAIN   Well then, young damsel?...

CINDERELLA   *(very cheerfully)* Just a moment, sir chamberlain. *(runs to where the* SISTERS *and* LADY LARK *are)* Take some of these oranges, all of you.

MARINA, ANTONIA AND LADY LARK   Thank you — thank you, princess. But that's plenty, thank you....

CINDERELLA   No, take some more. *(She keeps one orange for herself and happily begins to eat it, returning to center stage followed by the* CHAMBERLAIN.*)*

The COURTIERS *have waited, with signs of impatience, for* CINDERELLA *to finish distributing the fruit and now on tip-toe run up to her.*

FIRST COURTIER   Mademoiselle...

SECOND COURTIER   Princess...

FIRST COURTIER   *(gives the other a ferocious look)* Courtier!

Meanwhile TWO ENGAGING COUPLES, *one from the crowd and another from the terrace, also run up to her.*

FIRST COUPLE   *(together)* Celestial...

SECOND COUPLE   *(together)* Angel...

FIRST COURTIER   Just a word —

FIRST COUPLE   *(still in unison)* Help us, please!

SECOND COURTIER   One word from you to the prince —

SECOND COUPLE   *(still in unison)* Our happiness depends on you.

FIRST COUPLE   Listen to us —

Cinderella

First Courtier   *(with a thrust of the shoulder, he interposes)* We were here first.

A Third Courtier *has appeared majestically in the threshold of the door on the left, and from there he yells, louder than everyone.*

Third Courtier   *(yelling)* Don't pay attention to those two schemers, young lady.

First Courtier   Princess, princess…

The Two Couples   Listen to us a minute, Celestial Angel.

Little by little Cinderella, *unsure whether to be frightened or delighted, has found herself pushed into the group of musicians. She almost falls, and* Icarus *steadies her.*

Cinderella   Thank you. Oh, how's the viola?

Icarus   Very good.

Meanwhile Antonia *has done a turn around the stage and finds herself at the proscenium face to face with* Cinderella, *who, seeing her, takes a step toward her.*

Cinderella   Antonia.

Antonia   *(surprised)* How do you know my name?

Cinderella   *(after a moment of embarrassment)* The prince told me. He talked continuously about you.

Antonia   Oh, well then, what I wanted to ask you…

Cinderella   *(in a tone heavy with implication)* You will go to the terrace with Prince Charming.

Antonia   Thank you. Thank you.

All the Others   Wonderful.… Divine.… Us, too?… And Us?

Chamberlain   One at a time or I will clear the room.

Third Courtier   *(managing to make himself heard above all the others)* In a word, you should tell the prince that that appointment goes to me, because in three days I had twenty-six, and that one there *(indicating the first)* twenty-eight — it's true — but the last three he paid for. There's corruption. I can prove it. The Office of Protohistorian goes to me.

FIRST COURTIER   That's a lie. My twenty-eight were authentic, totally clean. The post goes to me. I'll show my documents.

The TWO COUPLES *and the* FIRST TWO COURTIERS *start to yell and scream over one another.*

CINDERELLA   *(plugging her ears)* I can't hear anything anymore!

CHAMBERLAIN   Silence! The prince.

As if by magic, everyone is silent.

CINDERELLA   Clever, sir chamberlain. But I didn't understand what they want.

CHAMBERLAIN   These gentlemen want a very prestigious appointment. According to the old customs, which function as laws, the high appointments are given to those who can prove they have received the most slaps in the face in the shortest amount of time. *(Confirms.)* Slaps.

CINDERELLA   *(pressing her hands together, scandalized)* Noo.... *(then looks at the* THREE COURTIERS *and bursts out laughing)*

THE TWO COUPLES   Celestial Angel, our parents oppose our engagement. If Prince Charming...

DIGNITARY   *(announcing from the upstage entrance)* His highness!

There is silence. All the postulates move to the side. The PRINCE *enters.*

CINDERELLA   *(goes to meet the* PRINCE) Why was everyone yelling before and now you could hear a fly fly?

PRINCE   *(vainly)* Because they are afraid of me.

CINDERELLA   You mustn't frighten people.

PRINCE   Did you see anything nice?

CINDERELLA   No, only ugly things.

PRINCE   Darling, because I was far away they seemed ugly. You knew to tell me what I had been waiting to hear, with words I didn't expect. I thank you, Celestial.

CINDERELLA   How difficultly you speak.

PRINCE   No, the language of the heart is easy. Stay close to me, Angel. Do you know why it took me so long to return?

CINDERELLA   But you came back right away.

PRINCE You are cruel. I was late because I spoke with the queen mother about you.

CINDERELLA Wait a minute, I…

CHAMBERLAIN (*coming upon them*) You are correct, mademoiselle, one minute. Because (*to the* PRINCE) over there the Spumante is ready, the ancestral Spumante.

CINDERELLA What is it? It must be something very beautiful.

CHAMBERLAIN (*loudly to the dinner guests, indicating the door upstage on the right*) Spumante.

EVERYONE *heads upstage and groups there, waiting for the* PRINCE *to pass.*

PRINCE (*heading upstage as well*) Something beautiful? But we ought not use the word "beautiful" anymore, except for you, Celestial.

PRINCE CHARMING *and* CINDERELLA *arrive upstage and the door opens. They exit to the right, followed by the* CROWD *and then the* MUSICIANS.

The CHAMBERLAIN *is left alone in the middle of the stage to see the crowd empty out. When everyone has gone, he begins to go as well. But from a corner upstage left, lifting a curtain, the* POLICE CHIEF *springs out and, running on tip-toes and putting a finger to his lips, reaches the* CHAMBERLAIN, *takes him by the arm and drags him toward the extreme left of the proscenium.*

CHAMBERLAIN Chief, the Spumante doesn't interest you?

POLICE CHIEF Psst…. Delicate information. A word, and then we'll run in there with an indifferent air.

CHAMBERLAIN Well, out with it!

Throughout, the noise of the crowd, talking and drinking, is heard.

POLICE CHIEF (*very mysterious, throughout the exchange*) Have you figured it out?

CHAMBERLAIN What?

POLICE CHIEF Who that woman is?

CHAMBERLAIN No.

POLICE CHIEF She's a spy.

CHAMBERLAIN Come on!

POLICE CHIEF Suspecting it, first thing, I ran outside. Search, investigate, reason. The stranger, dressed as she is, could not have come on the pedestrian path, which is a footpath in ruins. She had to have come in a carriage, on the main road. I ran to the end of the road. No sign of tracks — neither of wheels nor of horse hooves.

CHAMBERLAIN Well then?

POLICE CHIEF *(dramatic)* She didn't leave a trace! Characteristic of an expert criminal. Not a footprint of a single four-legged creature, nor a groove from a wheel.

CHAMBERLAIN And what happened to them, the horses and carriage?

POLICE CHIEF *(shrugs)* And what do I care? *(The* CHAMBERLAIN *is shocked.)* You're asking the wrong question. I was not looking for the horses or the carriage, I was looking for the tracks. You have to ask me what happened to the tracks.

CHAMBERLAIN That's right. Well, then?

POLICE CHIEF It's crystal clear. She destroyed them.

CHAMBERLAIN *(uninterested)* Ah.

POLICE CHIEF What do you mean, "Ah"? It would have taken time. I examined maybe a half a mile: nothing. But get worked up about it!

CHAMBERLAIN I'm worked up.

POLICE CHIEF Have no fear. *(slowly)* The traces of her coming don't exist *(pronouncing each syllable)* because she didn't come.

CHAMBERLAIN But if everyone saw her?

POLICE CHIEF She didn't come because *(whispering)* she was already here.

CHAMBERLAIN Here?

POLICE CHIEF I mean in the palace. For a week, a month. Hidden in a garret? A cellar? Who knows?

CHAMBERLAIN *(a beat, then suddenly)* Excellency, the ritual cannot be interrupted for this.

POLICE CHIEF   On the contrary.

CHAMBERLAIN   In five minutes —

POLICE CHIEF   *(mysteriously)* That's all it will take to show you.... *(backs up toward the corner on the left from which he sprung before)*

CHAMBERLAIN   *(intrigued, he follows with his eyes)* Crab walk?

POLICE CHIEF   *(having arrived upstage he turns, lifts the curtain half way up, calls inside, quietly)* Psstt....

Coming out from behind the curtain is a MAN *wrapped in a black cloak arranged so as to hide the bottom half of his face. On his head is a romantic broad-brimmed hat lowered to cover his forehead. All that can be seen is his eyes.*

CHAMBERLAIN   Who is it?

CLOAKED MAN   It's me. *(unwraps himself and takes off his hat with a musketeer's salute)*

CHAMBERLAIN   The maestro!

MAESTRO   Himself. Always and everywhere. In the service of her majesty the queen mother, who on the nights of grand parties, even remaining in her room, avails of my work for the arrangement of the royal tresses.

POLICE CHIEF   And I, who know everything, kept him behind in order to have some precious information. *(sottovoce)* Follow me, maestro, to that doorway. *(On tip-toe he pulls the* MAESTRO *toward the door through which the* PRINCE *and* GUESTS *exited. He opens it cautiously and positions* MAESTRO ADEMARO.*)* Look from here without letting them see you. Look at the little lady next to the prince who is dipping the mandarin in her Spumante. Strange behavior! Observe in silence.... Done?... Come *(pulls him away, closes the door quietly, and takes the* MAESTRO *back to where the* CHAMBERLAIN *has remained waiting)* Now speak. Did you do her hair?

MAESTRO   *(mystified and ecstatic)* No.

POLICE CHIEF   Who could have done her hair? *(He looks with a clever air at the* CHAMBERLAIN.*)*

MAESTRO *(inspired)* Only two people in the entire universe. Either me, or God. I didn't do her hair. God did.

CHAMBERLAIN There we have it.

POLICE CHIEF *(annoyed)* Like hell! These responses that are…that are…

CHAMBERLAIN Incorporeal…

POLICE CHIEF …don't get us anywhere. We are practical. We are realists. A more precise response would give me evidence enough.

MAESTRO *(severe)* Chief, you lack a sense of mystery. Your investigations ignore the lofty and the first causes.[3] For this reason your work can only function on an earthly level. Who fixed the tresses of the forests and the comets? Who gave the horse's mane its wave? Who put the crest on the phoenix's head? *(struck by an idea)* Oh, divine light! And who can guarantee you that she, who we take for a woman, isn't the fabled phoenix, come to us in the form of damsel?

CHAMBERLAIN *(amused)* I like it, I like it. *(to the* CHIEF*)* My friend, the phoenix flies. It doesn't leave tracks like a horse. That explains everything.

POLICE CHIEF One moment. I'm thinking. To fly, one needs wings. Where did she leave them, the wings?

MAESTRO *(mockingly, to the* CHIEF*)* Go look in the cloak room.

CHAMBERLAIN That's it.

POLICE CHIEF *(offended)* I'm surprised at you, chamberlain. You who are not interested in my scientific investigation. You're getting all wrapped up in a hypothesis that is completely… completely…

MAESTRO Lyrical, chief. Under the uniform of a chamberlain can beat the heart of a poet.

POLICE CHIEF *(purposefully offensive)* But not of a hair stylist!

MAESTRO The hair stylist is the fullest realization of the poet. I can't grant you anything other than my time, gentlemen. Cherish my revelation, if you can manage it. If you're not capable, shelve the

---

3. Here is yet another apparent recourse to philosophy, in this case Aristotle's reflections on causality.

case, as is your custom. I have to go. Berenice's tresses await me. Goodbye. *(With a new grand gesture, he puts the cloak and hat back on and then exits from where he entered.)*

CHAMBERLAIN   The five minutes have passed, and....

POLICE CHIEF   *(desperate)* But I can't investigate the sky.

CHAMBERLAIN   Stick to the ground. I have to give the order to start the mid quadrille. We are just in time. *(starts to go)*

POLICE CHIEF   *(keeping him)* But I need to take his highness aside and warn him…

CHAMBERLAIN   You are crazy! If you tell him of this suspicion, he'll have you hanged!

POLICE CHIEF   You tell him.

CHAMBERLAIN   *(dignified)* Don't cause trouble. I'm going. *(Runs to the door on the right and from there towards the inside, yelling:)* Ladies and gentlemen: the grand mid quadrille.

Voices from the inside grow and come nearer, while the POLICE CHIEF *mysteriously exits from where he came.*

PRINCE   *(entering with* CINDERELLA *on his arm)* Come, my adored one.

And the GUESTS *enter behind them.*

CINDERELLA   *(mildly excited)* Come here, come there. It's like walking around a big city, a countryside with lots of suns everywhere — don't you hear the bumble-bees flying about? You hear, but don't see them, and there's always something new to be done. The spumante was good, but why did they call us: "Ladies and gentlemen"? Why did they call us?

PRINCE   For the grand mid quadrille.

Everyone has re-entered. The MUSICIANS, *from their area, re-enter as well.*

CINDERELLA   Oh, this must be something beautiful, too. What is it?

PRINCE   Everything you do by my side seems beautiful.

CHAMBERLAIN   *(at the proscenium, facing the scene, continues to give orders)* The first four choose.

CINDERELLA *(to the* PRINCE*)* You didn't answer me, what is the mid quadrille?

PRINCE My God, the quadrille is…a quadrille.

CINDERELLA *(imitating him)* And the mid is…a mid. *(sighing)* But I don't know it. I won't know how to do this beautiful thing. I'll be very unhappy.

PRINCE Just walk straight ahead holding hands, then dance a moment, then turn, then walk again. Basically, I will lead you, just stay close to me.

CINDERELLA *(obstinate)* But why is it called "mid"?

CHAMBERLAIN *(hurrying)* Your highness' choice?

PRINCE Mine and the Celestial's, you mean. *(to* CINDERELLA*)* And to make four, we still need one man and one woman. Choose the woman. For example…

CINDERELLA *(enthused)* Woman? There *(calls)* Antonia! *(to the* PRINCE*)* It really needs to be Antonia.

ANTONIA *has run right to them.*

PRINCE As for the man…

CINDERELLA Me, me. I'll choose everyone. So much to do. *(She looks around.)*

PRINCE *(suggesting quietly)* That dignitary.

CINDERELLA *(She looks at him a moment and then bursts out laughing; suddenly, still laughing, she runs toward the musicians, takes* ICARUS *by the hand and drags him over to the* PRINCE*.)* Here's the man.

PRINCE *(embarrassed)* Really…

CINDERELLA He didn't bring it. He didn't bring it. I really wanted to see if he would be afraid to leave his viola.

ICARUS *(attempting to leave)* I can't…

PRINCE See.

CINDERELLA No, no. *(keeping* ICARUS*)* I really want to see him despair because he is away from his viola. Come on, the chamberlain says we have to hurry.

Cinderella

Meanwhile eight couples arrange themselves in two lines, and they wait behind the four people not yet organized (the Prince, Cinderella, Antonia, Icarus). *All the others in the room are likewise arranged and the* Chamberlain *runs here and there organizing them better.*

Chamberlain It's late!

Cinderella *quickly and paying no mind to the impatient gestures of the* Prince, *places* Antonia *on his right and joins their hands, then puts herself on his left, taking his hand, and with her own left hand takes* Icarus*'s right. And thus the* Prince*'s line is made.*

Prince But not like this.... *(tries to disengage himself to change the arrangement, but neither* Cinderella *nor* Antonia *will move)*

Chamberlain Is everybody ready? Is the music ready?

From various parts of the room in various tones, "Ready, ready, ready...." The Musicians *strike a big chord to signal their readiness.*

Cinderella The chamberlain! What is he waiting for?

Chamberlain Attention. *(With his arm raised, and as if he's listening, he shows in fact that he is waiting for something. After about ten seconds of complete silence, from outside and high above, a bell chimes.)* "One." Go!

The music begins and the three lines (in the lead, the Prince*'s line) begin to advance, walking rhythmically along the proscenium, from right to left. They're doing similar movements all over the stage.*

Second chime.

Chamberlain Two.

Cinderella *(walking in step)* How fun. It's like we're soldiers.

Third chime.

Chamberlain Three.

Prince *(bowing to* Cinderella *as if he is telling her an intimate secret)* When we arrive there, we turn to the right.

Fourth chime.

Chamberlain Four.

Cinderella But what kind of bell is that?

Courtiers Long live Prince Charming!

EVERYONE Long may he live!

Fifth chime.

CHAMBERLAIN Five.

COURTIERS Long live the Celestial Angel!

EVERYONE Long may she live!

CINDERELLA Oh no, that time I shouldn't have said it!

Sixth chime.

CHAMBERLAIN Six! Turn.

CINDERELLA *moves away from the* PRINCE *and gets in position to dance with* ICARUS. ANTONIA *does the same toward the* PRINCE, *and thus with all the other couples.*

Seventh chime.

CHAMBERLAIN Seven.

PRINCE Do you see it wasn't supposed to be this way?

But everyone dances, pulling PRINCE CHARMING *and* ANTONIA *along.*

Eighth chime.

CHAMBERLAIN Eight.

CINDERELLA *(to* ICARUS, *with whom she is dancing)* That noise irritates me, will it go on very long?

ICARUS What noise?

Ninth chime.

CHAMBERLAIN Nine.

ICARUS Oh, the bell. Three more strokes. They're the strokes of midnight.

CINDERELLA *(screams)* Ah! *(She stops for a moment, petrified.)*

PRINCE *(who continues to watch* CINDERELLA *as he dances with* ANTONIA, *stops instantly, too, and thus everyone else does as well)* What happened?

Tenth chime.

CHAMBERLAIN Ten.

Cinderella

CINDERELLA *(with an even sharper scream, lifts her hands to her head, backs away from* ICARUS *and, cutting through the crowd, makes for the stairs upstage.)* Nobody move. Goodbye, goodbye.

Eleventh chime.

CHAMBERLAIN   Eleven.

CINDERELLA *is already on the steps, behind her the people in a tumult. She climbs three stairs, on the last she trips and is about to fall but catches herself and pushes the door wide open. She disappears, and the door slams shut behind her. All of this has happened very quickly. In the surprise and confusion no one stopped her (only the* CHAMBERLAIN *and the* MUSICIANS *kept doing their job). The* PRINCE *reaches the stairs, and pushes the door open, shouting, "Angel!" the people scream "Angel," "Celestial."*

The twelfth chime sounds and breaking through the tumult is heard,

CHAMBERLAIN   Midnight!

as the episode ends.

End of Act Two

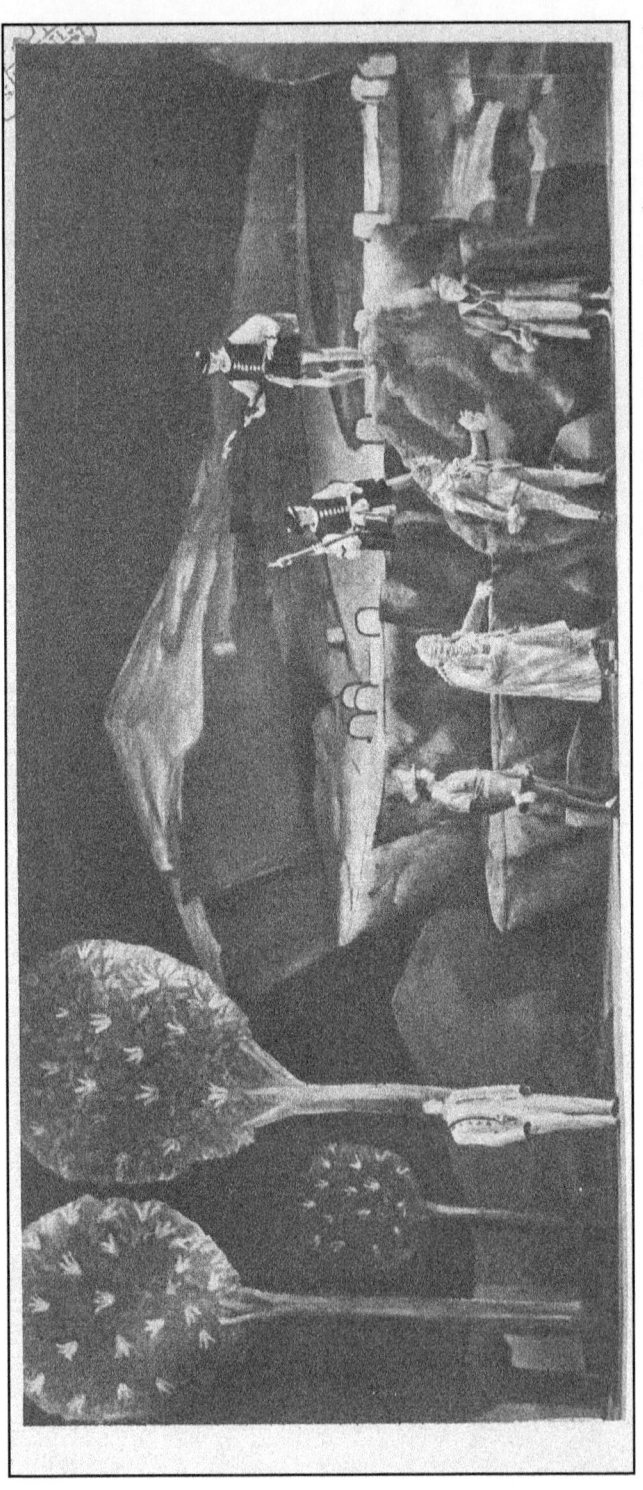

Act Three, Episode Four, in the 1942 Maggio Musicale Fiorentino debut production of *Cinderella*, directed by Corrado Pavolini. Scenario 11.6 (June 1942): 205. Courtesy of the Biblioteca Nazionale, Roma.

Cinderella

ACT THREE

Episode Four

The scene is divided lengthwise by an embankment, at the top of which is a road. Backdrop of columns. On the near side of the embankment, downstage left, are some trees, resembling the beginning of a forest, which continue into the wings. The rest is an abandoned, rocky clearing, which narrows into a footpath that disappears off to the right. From the road above down to where the clearing becomes the footpath, the embankment is broken by a steep cliff that essentially puts the road above in communication with the lower half of the scene.

A starry night without a moon.

When the episode begins, a few seconds of silence. Then from offstage, upstage left, comes a distant shouting, dispersed in various directions, mixed with quiet blasts of a very distant bugle, like those of people searching the area around the hills. The sounds disappear. Then a few isolated, far off voices call, "Princess...."

Pause. Then, again from offstage left, but this time further downstage, the PRINCE's *voice is heard calling, "Angeeeellll, Celestial Angel." Other* VOICES *echo him — "Celestial" — and then fade. Silence.*

CINDERELLA *enters the upstage road from the left, dressed as at the beginning of the play (apron and clogs, disheveled). She goes a few paces with great effort, then sits on the edge of the cliff, gasping for breath. Suddenly she lifts her head, frightened, listens, and looks off to the left. Voices from that direction, still far upstage but nearer in distance, can be heard.*

Instantly CINDERELLA *forces herself up, panic-stricken, looks down toward the clearing and is resolved. She begins to lower herself carefully down the cliff, using her hands to help.*

CINDERELLA   *(climbing down)* No...no.... I don't want them to find me, to see me this way. *(She stops halfway and listens.)* I don't hear them anymore. *(Begins again, arrives below. She drops to the ground, with her back against a rock.)* Who knows how far I've walked. Actually, maybe only a little. I'm still far away. *(Pause. She covers her face with her hands, breathing hard at first and then more slowly. It seems as if she's dozing off, then her breathing becomes sobs that threaten to suffocate her. She cries desperately with* her head in her hands. *Slowly she calms down. She takes off her clogs and looks at them, claps them together and is frightened by the loud noise they make. She looks around again. She looks at her feet and touches them. Then, with both clogs in one hand, she begins to speak again.)* What will the fairy godmother do now? My dear godmother, how could I forget? And you told me. One, two, three, and I didn't understand. I didn't understand anything anymore. I was crazy. Even before that, in that big room, the whole time I didn't think about my godmother even once. I was good with the sisters and stepmother, but I was bad with you, who loved me. You comforted me, you taught me many things, you taught me the stars. *(looks at the sky)* They're all here. Just last night I tried to count them. It seems like a lot of time has passed, *(looks slowly around)* it seems like then I was a child and now I'm grown up. Maybe when you grow up you become bad. I danced, I drank spumante, I had fun walking like soldiers. I was stupid. Maybe when you grow up you become stupid. And I didn't think. I didn't pay attention, not even when the bell kept ringing, and six, seven.... *(shivers)* Now I'd be in bed. I would have told her everything. I'd be sleeping. Instead, now...I can't take it anymore. It's hard to walk in these. *(looking at the clogs)* Luckily no one can see me. Only the stars see me. *(looks again at the sky)* So many. Before I didn't see so many. She sure knows all their names, even of those that once were there and are no more. One day I won't be here anymore either. Maybe I'll go up there, like all of those people who were once men and women and then became stars in the sky. And my Godmother will see that there's one more, and only she will know that that one is the Cinderella star, the silly girl who forgot to obey. Where will I go? Maybe in the middle of those little ones that are blinking. It must be really cold up there. I'd like to try to walk a little bit. This one must go into the city, too. *(Indicates the footpath. With great effort she starts off again.)*

But now a little closer (up above) some of those voices can be heard. CINDERELLA, *frightened, leans against the rock, frozen. A* BUGLER *with bugle around his neck arrives on the road from the left, as does a* SCOUT *with a lit torch.*

BUGLER   *(looks below, and then turns upstage and yells toward offstage)* Nothing here, above or below! What? Yes, send two on

Cinderella

the path. It's the last one. Stay there until they return. I'll go into the forest and wait for his highness. *(frightened motion by* CINDERELLA*) (to the* SCOUT*)* You stay here as guard — *(begins to descend the cliff, but stops immediately, calling to him again)* You, just a minute, come and give me some light. *(The* SCOUT *runs and stays at the top of the cliff, lighting it below, but the light doesn't reach* CINDERELLA, *who clings ever more desperately to the rock, while the* BUGLER *continues to descend.)*

Voices are heard, from down left — from inside the forest. CINDERELLA *barely breathes. The* BUGLER, *with one last jump, arrives below, grazing* CINDERELLA *without seeing her, and goes to the left to wait by the trees. The* SCOUT *above returns to his post. The voices below approach. The* BUGLER, *turning toward the forest, gives a bugle blow. From the left, passing through the trees, enters the sullen* PRINCE, *preceded by a* SECOND SCOUT *with lit torch and accompanied by the* CHAMBERLAIN, *followed by* ICARUS, *who remains apart, leaning against a tree.*

CHAMBERLAIN Here, highness, is the limit of the holding, a perfect place to rest a minute. I am very tired.

PRINCE I'm surprised at you. I am not tired, so you shouldn't be.

CHAMBERLAIN *(immediately)* I'm not tired, highness. Not at all. I feel like we just left the palace.

PRINCE *(to the* BUGLER*)* Speak.

BUGLER Highness, on the footpaths up there, nothing. Right now they're combing the last one. If they don't find her there…but it'll be difficult.…

CHAMBERLAIN And if she wasn't found in any of the palace gardens.…

PRINCE *(severe)* Then?

CHAMBERLAIN The search will have been in vain, and we will be forced into a renunciation.

PRINCE *(irate)* What do you mean, "renunciation"?

CHAMBERLAIN *(immediately)* Bitter, highness, a bitter renunciation.

PRINCE *(firmly)* If you don't find her in — *(He's interrupted by the sound of a bugle offstage in the distance. Everyone looks up.)*

SCOUT *(up above, he listens toward offstage)* What? Alright. *(calling downstage)* Nothing on the last path, highness.

PRINCE *(to the* CHAMBERLAIN*)* It was a given. It could only lead to the city. *(indicating the street above on the right)*

BUGLER Excuse me, highness. There's also this one, which is shorter. But it's almost impassible.

CHAMBERLAIN Oh, oh. Could a little lady, dressed like a cloud, shod in flower petals, walk on that path?

BUGLER Impossible.

CHAMBERLAIN I told you, *(definitive)* bitter renunciation.

PRINCE To the city! *(to the* CHAMBERLAIN*)* Gather everybody up there, go out in the carriages, make sure that…oh! *(Suddenly the* SECOND SCOUT*'s torch lights up* CINDERELLA*, and he sees her.)* Who's that there? Who are you?

CINDERELLA *(frightened, she tries to take a step backward, barely staying on her feet)* Me? I don't know, really.

PRINCE You haven't seen anyone pass by here?

CINDERELLA No, no.

PRINCE A young girl dressed in pearl? Beautiful?

CINDERELLA No, no.

PRINCE Have you been here a long time?

CINDERELLA Time? I don't know. I don't know really.

PRINCE *(shrugs)* Are you a beggar?

CINDERELLA I don't know. I don't know. Ah maybe…that's it.

PRINCE *(to the* OTHERS*)* She's an idiot. And so ugly. *(to* CINDERELLA*)* Why do you have your clogs in your hands? Clogs are for feet.

CINDERELLA I don't know. I don't know really. Maybe, yes.

PRINCE She's insane. Let's go, chamberlain.

CHAMBERLAIN Just a moment, I think I heard a bugle.

PRINCE From where?

CHAMBERLAIN From there, no, over there….

PRINCE *(to the* BUGLER*)* Did you hear it?

CHAMBERLAIN *desperately signals to the* BUGLER *to say "yes."*

BUGLER   Highness, no…I mean, there's a headwind.

PRINCE   (*to the* SECOND SCOUT) And you?

SECOND SCOUT   (*who saw the signal*) Highness, yes. One sound only. Taaa…. (*imitating the sound*)

And a real bugle call is heard, from behind the trees but still not very close.

CHAMBERLAIN   There, the wind has become favorable. Favorable, and kind.

PRINCE   (*to the* SECOND SCOUT) Make a sign with the torch so they see it through the trees.

SECOND SCOUT *raises the torch and waves it toward the left.*

PRINCE   But who stayed behind?

CHAMBERLAIN   No one. Fresh arrivals.

PRINCE   Let's wait for them.

CHAMBERLAIN   Waiting, waiting. Allow me to suggest that your majesty sit down. (*He cleans a rock for him with his coattails.*)

The PRINCE *sits down, mechanically.*

CHAMBERLAIN   (*sitting on the ground, sighing with satisfaction*) Strange fates of men.

BUGLER AND SECOND SCOUT   (*together*) They're coming.

Entering from the left, the POLICE CHIEF *accompanied by a* SECOND BUGLER *with lit torch.*

POLICE CHIEF   Highness, an important discovery.

PRINCE   Did you find her?

POLICE CHIEF   Highness, no, but…

PRINCE   Well, then, nothing is important.

POLICE CHIEF   I mean, we didn't really find her, that is, not all of her, but…

PRINCE   (*getting up, agitated*) What do you mean not all of her? Hurry.

CHAMBERLAIN, *seeing the* PRINCE *get up, with great effort gets up too.*

POLICE CHIEF Scouring the palace, right on the threshold of the grand ballroom, which was empty, I stumbled on an object, which I collected right away. Examining it, I followed right in your tracks to deliver it to you. From the beginning —

PRINCE *(impatient)* What object?

POLICE CHIEF *(takes a packet from his breast pocket, unwraps it calmly, and out falls a slipper)* This slipper, color of pearl, has certainly been lost by the fugitive.

PRINCE *(grabs it from him)* Certainly it's hers. Dearest, *(exalting it)* here was your foot, your adored foot….

POLICE CHIEF Left.

PRINCE Her left foot. And now where is the right? And all of her? *(inspired)* Ah, we have to find her, right away, even if she is at the ends of the earth.

POLICE CHIEF According to my calculations she shouldn't be at the ends of the earth, but at furthest, in the city.

PRINCE Well then, to the city!

POLICE CHIEF Keep in mind that she will be in disguise. *(sententious and mysterious)* All fugitives disguise themselves.

PRINCE Hurry to the city! Celestial is there. She will be mine! Wake up every house. Make an announcement. All the girls of the city, every last one, must present themselves in their doorways. We will try this young fairy's slipper on each of them. The person whom it fits, whatever her disguise is, has to be her. Her.

CHAMBERLAIN Stupendous.

PRINCE And the announcement will conclude: The prince will marry her, make her princess and in her time queen, the young girl who is able to wear this jewel, this flower.

CHAMBERLAIN Announcement! Announcement!

PRINCE Go, without delay. Put together the honor guard and buglers in uniform.

CHAMBERLAIN And the dress carriage for your highness and the dignitaries.

PRINCE   Of course…ah no, for me, no! *(struck by a sudden idea)* I won't go in the carriage, but on a horse, on a white horse. I will be much more handsome.

CHAMBERLAIN   A white horse.

POLICE CHIEF   But if first —

PRINCE   *(impatient)* You can tell me at the palace. Go on.

BUGLER   *(to the* SCOUT *up above)* Join the others and wait for his highness.

The SCOUT *exits upstage left.*

POLICE CHIEF   Permit me…

The PRINCE, *(ignoring him)* SECOND SCOUT, TWO BUGLERS *and the* CHAMBERLAIN *leave the forest. The* POLICE CHIEF *— who hasn't yet resolved to follow the* PRINCE *—* ICARUS, *and* CINDERELLA *— who hasn't moved a muscle — remain on stage.* ICARUS *detaches himself from the tree.*

POLICE CHIEF   *(seeing him, desperately confides)* They didn't search along the footpath. The most interesting investigation. But he didn't give me a chance to speak. And he's waiting for me. *(motioning toward the path)* There —

ICARUS   They said for a lady dressed like that it would be impractical.

POLICE CHIEF   Fugitives love the impractical. And even if she went by the good road, you know that there's a cliff worse than this one ahead. The fugitive could have followed the carriage road for a while *(indicates it)* and between anxiety and darkness fallen down there. *(starting to move)* God, the prince is waiting for me…. They often find detached limbs and scraps of clothing from fugitives. In this case I would find it very costly to present to his highness with the remains of his darling. *(sighs)* But I have to join him. And there he's not going to let me speak either.

ICARUS   *(lit up by a sudden idea, after a quick look towards* CINDERELLA*)* Your honor… do you say "your honor" to a police chief?

POLICE CHIEF   "Excellency."

ICARUS   Pardon me. Excellency, I know this area stone for stone, all the way to the city. Trust me to travel it.

POLICE CHIEF   *(correcting him)* Scour it. And the limbs? The possible limbs?

ICARUS   Right, as you go to join the prince, send me a stretcher and four stretcher-bearers.

POLICE CHIEF   Both agile and robust.

ICARUS   If I find the limbs, I will have them sent to your office with the stretcher.

POLICE CHIEF   Marvelous. I better run. Don't move from here until they arrive.

ICARUS   No.

The POLICE CHIEF *rushes out stage left.* ICARUS *— as soon as he's moved away from the* POLICE CHIEF *— looks around, looks up at the road, listens. After making sure no one is nearby, runs to* CINDERELLA, *who after all the stress seems to be suddenly dozing off on the rock. He stops a few steps away from her, showing great respect.*

CINDERELLA   *(shakes herself and again behaves like she is being interrogated)* No, really, I didn't see anyone.

ICARUS   *(kneels in front of her)* Princess…

CINDERELLA   *(frightened)* What?

ICARUS   I recognized you. You were the girl at the ball who came down from heaven. You danced with me. Thank you.

CINDERELLA   No, no. I don't understand. What do you want from me?

ICARUS   I want to ask your forgiveness.

CINDERELLA   *(shocked)* For what?

ICARUS   For not letting you pluck the strings of my viola. Forgive me.

CINDERELLA   *(after a very brief pause, suddenly begins to laugh and clap her hands)* But it would have gone out of tune. You were right.

ICARUS   *(laughs, standing)* Now that you have forgiven me —

CINDERELLA   No, I didn't say anything. I don't know anything… no one has passed by here. *(looks at herself, shrinks into herself, ashamed)*

Cinderella

ICARUS You don't have to be ashamed of that dress…

CINDERELLA *(lifts her head, surprised; murmurs)* How did you figure it all out?

ICARUS …and I won't ask you why you're in disguise.

CINDERELLA *(lowering her eyes)* I'm not in disguise, like this.

ICARUS *(not catching what she said)* …and I won't ask you anything else. But I want to help you. The only thing you need to tell me is where you want to go. I know all of the roads. If you live in the city…

CINDERELLA Yes, yes.

ICARUS It's this road. *(indicates the footpath to the right)* Much shorter than that one. *(pointing above)*

CINDERELLA But this one is impossible. They said so.

ICARUS *(smiles)* I could do it blindfolded and carrying you in my arms.

CINDERELLA There's no need. I'm rested now. *(gets off of the rock, takes a step forward, but sways and is about to fall)*

ICARUS *(picks her up)* You're a feather.

CINDERELLA *(darkens again)* No, don't say that *(murmurs)* — they already said it.

ICARUS *(setting her on the square rock)* And here you can finally put yourself back together. *(smiling, indicates the clogs)*

CINDERELLA *(puts them back on and looks at her feet)* They're ugly. *(raising her head, she sighs)* We have to go.

ICARUS *(looks back, smiles wickedly)* There's time. First let's wait for one thing.

CINDERELLA For what?

ICARUS Didn't you hear what we said?

CINDERELLA Not everything, no. When the people came I was really, really scared, and when he talked to me, too, I was very afraid, but I was also very happy inside because he didn't recognize me like this. And I know I responded badly, but it was a little bit for real and a little bit pretending.

113

ICARUS You responded very well.

CINDERELLA Then for a little while I was confused. My head was spinning, and I couldn't hear anymore. But if you recognized me, why didn't you tell the prince, who looked so carefully with all those people?

ICARUS Because he should have recognized you himself.

CINDERELLA And how come you recognized me, and he didn't?

ICARUS They have other things to think about, big things.

CINDERELLA *(laughs)* But he thought about the slipper, which is a really little thing. I heard that for a minute…but let's not talk about it anymore.

ICARUS No, princess.

CINDERELLA *(sad)* I am not a princess, I am… *(looking at herself)* like this. But one has to have courage. Everyone is called by his own name. You, I mean, you, Mr…

ICARUS No, no, let's call each other by our first names.

CINDERELLA What's your name?

The questions and answers come more quickly.

ICARUS I'm Icarus, and you?

CINDERELLA Oh, it's one of those names that the fairy godmother knows, but I don't even remember my real name anymore because they call me…it's strange…they call me Cinderella.

ICARUS How beautiful it is, Cinderella, Cinderella.

CINDERELLA Oh, now I like it. The fairy godmother said so, too. There will come a moment —

ICARUS But who is this fairy?

CINDERELLA All these things at once, Icarus…we'll have time to tell them little by little.

ICARUS *(surprised)* What? When?

CINDERELLA *(surprised now, too)* It's true, when? Who knows what I meant.

ICARUS You meant that we will see each other again.

CINDERELLA Often?

Cinderella

ICARUS Always, Cinderella.

CINDERELLA Really? The fairy godmother, too? But you don't know who she is. She is my godmother, who teaches me the names of the stars and has me listen to the song of the earth.

ICARUS These are beautiful, precious things.

CINDERELLA You know music, Icarus. You would really like it. Last night from my terrace —

ICARUS In the city?

CINDERELLA Yes,…she told me, "look down and listen hard," and it was true. I looked down, and listening hard, I heard the earth's song. Do you want to try?

ICARUS Well then, if looking down and listening hard you hear the earth sing, looking up and listening hard you'll hear the sky sing.

CINDERELLA *(clapping her hands)* It's true. Should we try it?

ICARUS One minute. We have to be in the right place. *(He sits next to her, holds her, and cheek to cheek, they look toward the stars. Meanwhile we begin to hear, lightly and then little by little growing louder, a harmony from above.)* Where do we have to look?

CINDERELLA At a star. At that one, *(points)* not right at the star, but at that little empty space, see it? It's where I wanted to go when I was here alone and couldn't go on. I was desperate.

ICARUS Were you very frightened? Tell me about it.

CINDERELLA Shh. Don't you hear it, Icarus?

ICARUS I hear it, Cinderella.

CHORUS OF THE SKY

> From earth to stars
> the sky is full of thoughts that fly.
> On light wings
> through the air they bring
> new light to the last star.
> When that star appears
> the hearts of men will be
> just one heart in the sky.

The chorus's harmony continues softly in the background.

CINDERELLA Don't you think that all the stars are sisters?

ICARUS It seems like the sky is breathing.

CINDERELLA *(listening and almost accompanying it)* All one. All one.

The song has become a murmur and continues without interruption. Meanwhile, suddenly from the forest on the left,

FOUR VOICES *(calling)* Hey? Hey!

CINDERELLA *starts.*

ICARUS *(jumps to his feet and, keeping a hand on her head to reassure her, calls toward them)* Over here, over here.

FOUR STRETCHER-BEARERS *with an empty stretcher enter from the forest.*

ONE *(to* ICARUS*)* Police. The chief said to place ourselves at your command.

ICARUS Put that on the ground. *(to* CINDERELLA*)* Get up. Get on. In a half hour we will be in the city to await the court.

CINDERELLA But...

ICARUS *(puts a hand over her mouth, then he takes her by both hands, gets her up and has her sit on the stretcher. To the men)* She's light. That way. *(indicating the footpath)*

The FOUR STRETCHER-BEARERS *lift the stretcher and set out.* ICARUS, *toward the proscenium, accompanies the stretcher, holding* CINDERELLA'*s right hand. The stretcher glides into the path and goes off to the right, while the episode ends and the chorus is taken up again. It crescendos and then dies down, and this is enough to fill the time of the scene change.*

Episode Five

A square on the city limits. Backdrop of hills and countryside. On the right is Cinderella's house, with one floor and a terrace on the roof, the façade facing the audience. A front door with three or four steps, two symmetrical windows with the shutters closed. To the left are other houses, with their facades facing center.

Dawn. Throughout, the scene grows gradually brighter.

Cinderella

The stage is empty. Then, approaching sleigh bells can be heard, which cease offstage right. Immediately, LADY LARK, MARINA *and* ANTONIA *enter, as if coming from the carriage. They are still dressed for the ball, but a bit weary and disheveled. The* COACHMAN *follows them.* LADY LARK *turns to him.*

LADY LARK *(paying him)* There, good bye.

COACHMAN Thank you, but, my, the climb was tough. Good day. *(exits to the right)*

While the sleigh bells begin to ring and then quickly die out, LADY LARK *catches up with her daughters, who are entering the house.*

ANTONIA *(angry with* LADY LARK, *as if restarting an argument)* I will never forgive you!

LADY LARK For what?

ANTONIA For not wanting to go with the others and look for the princess, who promised to recommend me.

LADY LARK The carriage couldn't wait.

MARINA *(cattily, to* ANTONIA*)* Were we supposed to walk?

ANTONIA *shrugs her shoulders.*

LADY LARK *(knocks on the door and calls)* Cinderella!

MARINA It will take more than that for that groundhog to hear us.

But the window on the right opens immediately.

CINDERELLA *(appearing)* Welcome back!

LADY LARK Come down and let us in.

CINDERELLA I'll be right there. *(She retreats. The sound of her clogs on the stairs can be heard.)*

We hear bugle blasts from offstage right, still far away, and a confused buzz, quickly interrupted.

CINDERELLA *(opening the door)* Was it a lovely party?

LADY LARK What were those noises?

CINDERELLA What noises? Up until now it's been quiet.

ANTONIA *(digs one of the candied oranges from the ball out of her purse, to* CINDERELLA*)* Take this orange I have left over.

CINDERELLA Thank you. It's so lovely.

ANTONIA Eat it, sister.

MARINA (*to* ANTONIA) Let's go, I'm tired.

CINDERELLA *goes back inside. The bugles sound again, a bit closer, then silence falls.*

LADY LARK Those are the court buglers!

ANTONIA Maybe it's the prince come to look for me?

A HERALD *with bugle, followed by a crowd of* BOYS, *enters from the right. He looks around, then gives a bugle blast. From the center of the square he yells,*

HERALD Every house and every person, awake! Our prince is scouring the city. Every girl, of every age and condition, come out onto your doorsteps! Wear your slippers. Immediately.

The windows of the houses on the left open slightly.

MARINA (*to the* HERALD) Dressed like this, in our gowns?

HERALD (*ignoring her, yells*) Within five minutes. (*exits where he entered*)

BOYS (*of their own accord go knocking on all the doors, yelling*) Wake up! Wake up!

LADY LARK (*to the* BOYS) Go on, go on.

ANTONIA (*to* MARINA) There's no doubt. He's come for me.

MARINA (*nasty*) He's coming to look for the princess.

LADY LARK Go on, go up and change, hurry.

ALL THREE *enter the house, calling "Cinderella, where are you? Day clothes, right away!"*

BOYS Let's go meet him. (*They exit, right, marching like soldiers and singing the Ragamuffin chorus from the first act of* Carmen.)

TWO HOMELY GIRLS *appear on the doorstep of the first house on the left.*

HOMELY GIRLS Here we are. We are ready.

From the same door, their MAID, *rather pretty, joins them.*

MAID (*does a military salute*) Present!

Cinderella

HOMELY GIRLS You go away. What do you have to do with it? Go sweep the stairs.

MAID Prince's orders. The herald said, "of every condition."

The BOYS *come back, with others, and some other curious* PEOPLE.

BOYS The prince, the prince.

FIRST BOY He's at the green house. He'll be here in a few minutes.

SECOND BOY He was on horseback.

THIRD BOY On a white horse.

ALL BOYS *(imitating the* BUGLER*)* Taaa…taaa…

PEOPLE *appear in the windows of the other houses, but the doors remain closed.*

LADY LARK *(appears in the window on the right, looks, and then turning toward the inside yells)* Hurry up. The others are ready already.

MARINA'S VOICE Cinderella.…

ANTONIA'S VOICE No, me first. Cinderella.

BOY *(looking to the right)* The prince has gotten off his horse. He'll come up on foot.

The HERALD *re-enters, while* ANTONIA *and* MARINA *come out of the house in day dress, accompanied by* LADY LARK.

HERALD Silence! The prince!

Heartier bugle blasts from offstage. THREE BUGLERS *enter, then the* PRINCE *with the* CHAMBERLAIN *at his side carrying the slipper on a damask pillow; then a* COMMISSION OF FOUR DIGNITARIES *in fancy dress. At some distance various people, kept back by* GUARDS *with halberds.* ANTONIA, MARINA *and* LADY LARK *on one side, the* TWO HOMELY GIRLS *and the* MAID *on the other, rise to their feet.*

HERALD His highness orders you to be seated. *(The* SIX WOMEN *sit.)* Silence.

The BOYS *and the* PEOPLE *are silent.*

HERALD How many girls are there in this square?

TWO HOMELY GIRLS We're two here.

MAID And I'm three.

MARINA And us, two.

HERALD No one else? *(looking around)* Five.

CHAMBERLAIN *(to the* DIGNITARIES*)* But where is the local deputy commissioner?

DIGNITARY He stayed behind. *(looking toward the offstage)* No, there he is.

MAESTRO ADEMARO *enters from the right.*

ANTONIA The maestro! *(jumps to her feet)*

MARINA, LADY LARK, HOMELY GIRLS AND MAID *(get up, shouting)* Maestro....

MAESTRO Himself. Me.

HERALD Sit!

The SIX WOMEN *sit.*

HERALD Attention. The grand chamberlain speaks.

A bugle blast. General silence. The PRINCE *has remained in the middle of the square, sullen and distant.*

CHAMBERLAIN His highness our prince has called out this announcement throughout the city: that all of the girls here residing must try this slipper on their left foot. Here's the good part: the one whom this slipper fits will be the one we are searching for. And his highness will marry her, make her princess, then queen, and so on. *(murmurs in the crowd, various reactions from the* FIVE GIRLS*)* Attention. Every girl who has tried on the slipper, from the other end of the city up to this point, which if God wills it will be the end, has failed the test. Now it's down to the last five. It's time for the test. Next!

The crowd applauds. Meanwhile a group has formed downstage right. They watch and comment. Silence. The COMMISSION *lines up and begins to move toward the houses on the left. Whispered comments are heard.*

MAN *(to the person next to him)* They've invented this new way for a man to find a wife.

WOMAN And if the slipper doesn't fit anyone?

Cinderella

ANTONIA   (*to* MARINA) See? We know very well that the princess isn't any of them. *(indicating the three girls at the house on the left)* It's all a performance so the prince can arrive at me.

MARINA   Pfff. *(obviously suppresses a scornful smile)*

Very solemnly, the COMMISSION *arrives at the house on the left. The* PRINCE *remains in the middle of the square. The* GUARDS' *watchful eyes keep the* PEOPLE *and the* BOYS *upstage from coming too close.*

In the midst of the silence, the FIRST HOMELY GIRL *has taken off her slipper. The* CHAMBERLAIN, *placing the pillow cautiously on the ground and then a knee on it, tries the slipper on her foot. He turns to the* PRINCE, *emotionless.*

CHAMBERLAIN   Nothing.

FIRST HOMELY GIRL *is frozen in sadness. Murmurs.*

CHAMBERLAIN   *(does the same with the* SECOND HOMELY GIRL, *then turns to the* PRINCE) Nothing.

SECOND HOMELY GIRL   *(In a huff, she gets up.)* Let's go! *(tries to push the* FIRST *and the* MAID *inside)*

CHAMBERLAIN   *(immediately)* Wait! The third one.

SECOND HOMELY GIRL   But she's the servant.

CHAMBERLAIN   The announcement says, "Of every condition."

The TWO HOMELY GIRLS *enter the house. The* CHAMBERLAIN *begins to try with the* MAID, *and while he does he looks at her with a kind but superior smile, tries delicately to force the slipper on her foot, but then he turns, shamefaced.*

CHAMBERLAIN   Nothing. *(He gets up.)*

The BOYS *whistle and shout from upstage. The* GUARDS *lower the halberds threateningly; the* HERALD *yells, "Silence." The* COMMISSION *moves toward Cinderella's house. The* CHAMBERLAIN, *seeing a* PRETTY YOUNG WOMAN *appear on the balcony of one of the other houses on the left, stops.*

CHAMBERLAIN   And you, you're not coming down to be measured?

PRETTY YOUNG WOMAN   I'm married.

CHAMBERLAIN   Are you sure?

PRETTY YOUNG WOMAN   Quite sure.

CHAMBERLAIN   That's a shame.

The COMMISSION *starts off again toward Cinderella's house, where* ANTONIA *and* MARINA *wait on the steps.* LADY LARK *moves off to the side. The* PRINCE *remains silent in the middle of the square. Now all he does is turn toward Cinderella's house and then, as before, remains immobile.*

CHAMBERLAIN   (*to the* TWO SISTERS) Which one of you two is older?

ANTONIA *laughs.*

MARINA   (*disappointed*) I am...by a little. (*She takes off her left slipper. Some of the people sneer.*)

CHAMBERLAIN   (*hurriedly does as he did with the others*) Nothing.

MARINA   My feet are swollen from all that dancing last night.

CHAMBERLAIN   (*to* ANTONIA) Last. (*with gallantry*) And so the last shall be first. (*He hesitates over* ANTONIA'*s foot*) Allow me, mademoiselle, your stocking should be pulled a bit higher.... Like this.... I could have sworn...my God... (*turns toward the* PRINCE *for encouragement, but he irritably avoids his look*) I don't know what to do. It doesn't fit.

ANTONIA   In truth, the classic type's no good. But if you try hard...

CHAMBERLAIN   (*tries again murmuring something unintelligible; disappointed, he decides to turn to the* PRINCE) Nothing. (*And slowly, sadly, he gets up.*)

SOME VOICES   (*here and there*) Shame...what a shame...that's too bad. (*They die out.*)

CHAMBERLAIN   (*to the* PRINCE, *who in lethargy seems neither to hear nor see anything; desolately*) She was the last one.

A moment of general confusion and subdued murmurs, quickly drowned out by the sudden sound of ANTONIA'*s voice.*

ANTONIA   (*getting up*) Highness, I understand. You came for me, and you want me to realize it for myself. The princess has fled, and you won't find her anymore. Highness... (*Takes a step forward and waits, poised to accept his proposal*)

PRINCE   (*doesn't look at her; slowly raises his hand; in total silence, to the* CHAMBERLAIN, *almost whispering*) No winner.

Cinderella

CHAMBERLAIN *(loudly to the crowd)* No winner. The slipper remains a widow.

Whispered comments among the group on the right, a murmur a bit louder from the folks upstage, this time dominated by MARINA's *shrill voice.*

MARINA *(cattily, holding back but not hiding her resentment, to the* CHAMBERLAIN*)* You forgot someone.

CHAMBERLAIN But who?

MARINA There's still another girl to try. Who knows if his highness hasn't finally met his worthy match.

CHAMBERLAIN But who is it? Where is she?

MARINA *(rather scornfully)* Cinderella.

Everyone laughs.

MARINA This time they're laughing more than they did at me.

CHAMBERLAIN Where is this — I didn't catch her name.

TWO OR THREE OF THE PEOPLE *(making a ruckus, to* MARINA*)* Is she upstairs?

MARINA Yes, yes. *(calling toward the house)* Cinderella…

TWO OR THREE Let's go get her. *(They enter the house, cackling.)*

CHAMBERLAIN *(to* MAESTRO ADEMARO*)* Deputy Commissioner, do we have to try her?

MAESTRO Certainly. It's necessary, legal, cruel, definitive.

The TWO OR THREE *return, dragging a reluctant and frightened* CINDERELLA.

CINDERELLA No, not me. *(ashamed, her hair more disheveled and hanging in her face than ever; her clogs noisy)*

VOICES OF THE PEOPLE *(upstage)* They're trying with Cinderella.

Everybody laughs. Suddenly CINDERELLA *laughs too, then remains inert.* ANTONIA *and* MARINA *move off the steps, and the* TWO OR THREE *make* CINDERELLA *sit there, removing her left clog. The mocking continues.*

CHAMBERLAIN Herald!

HERALD *(loudly, to the people)* Silence. *(and he blasts his bugle)*

CHAMBERLAIN *(lowering his head, rests the pillow on the ground and takes up the same position)* We respect — to the point of absurdity — the order of the law, which is the order of the prince. Silence.

General silence. The slipper slides right onto CINDERELLA*'s foot.*

CHAMBERLAIN *(shocked and dismayed)* It's on. It's on...perfectly. *(turns)* Highness...

PRINCE *(jolted out of his lethargy, he looks from a distance, and then hurries to the* CHAMBERLAIN, *looks closely)* It's true...but this... chamberlain.... It seems to me...

CHAMBERLAIN *(mortified)* Highness, yes. *(gets up, nervously swinging the pillow back and forth)*

PRINCE Tonight, under the embankment, the...

CHAMBERLAIN The idiot, exactly. Strange fates of men!

EVERYONE, *the* COMMISSION *and the* PEOPLE, *is speechless. The second window opens for the first time, and there the* FAIRY GODMOTHER *appears.*

GODMOTHER *(showing the other slipper)* And this is the other, the right. *(Everyone looks at her a moment in silence. In the* FAIRY GODMOTHER*'s raised hand, the slipper radiates light.)*

PEOPLE A miracle! A miracle! *(Many get on their knees.)*

GODMOTHER Maestro, put this one on her as well. *(throws it and he catches it in the air)* And why don't you, with a touch of your magic hands, show everyone her real hair? Aren't shoes and hair enough to render someone recognizable?

MAESTRO Even just the hair. *(He's put the shoes on* CINDERELLA *and now gets up and with two hands holds back her hair.)* Twisting this, turning this other in a vortex, marrying one to the other, always deferring to the natural arc of the head and fastening it, like this, with a knot worthy of Solomon, there.... *(Continuing the sentence, he moves* CINDERELLA *away and examines her, who during all of this has remained partially hidden. Her face appears white and luminous as the* FAIRY GODMOTHER *made it in Act One.)* There, out of a wretched girl we have made —

PRINCE *(enthusiastically interrupts)* A princess. The angel. The celestial. My lady for all time. What the announcement said will be carried out without delay. So, court, so, people, my bride.

And you, you, my lady, and my heart told me, even in the dark, in poor clothes —

CINDERELLA *(threatening him with her pointed finger)* Come, come, let's not tell lies, highness. That's not right.

PRINCE *(condescending)* ...my heart told me. I ask forgiveness from you, my bride, from you who will be queen, so now, right away —

CINDERELLA   Excuse me, handsome prince, for a girl Prince Charming must remain Prince Charming. When he is king, he doesn't matter any more. Who ever heard of King Charming? And so Cinderella must remain Cinderella.

PRINCE   But all people grow and change. Tonight, at my side, you grew and were no longer Cinderella. You truly were an angel come down from heaven.

CINDERELLA   And after a while, it was necessary to let that angel go back to heaven. If not, the angel cries. But Cinderella doesn't cry and is happy to be on earth.

PRINCE   And the poor prince?

CINDERELLA   The poor prince won't be poor anymore if he forgets everything that was perhaps just a dream, and he too returns *(in a tone heavy with implication)* to how he was when I first found him.

PRINCE *(surprised)* When?

CINDERELLA   When you were dancing peacefully and hadn't yet begun to dream. The prince must become king, and the king needs a more queenly bride. I know who would be good.... *(She turns to call* ANTONIA*)* Antonia, don't you remember that I promised to send you to the terrace?

PRINCE *(a little indignant)* But my personal desire....

CINDERELLA   I see it in your eyes, Prince Charming. *(Having taken* ANTONIA *by the hand, leading her to the* PRINCE, *she turns to the* PEOPLE.*)* Look how beautiful they are, our princely couple.

PEOPLE   Long live the prince! Long live Princess Antonia! Long live...

VOICE   And the noble mother-in-law!

Massimo Bontempelli

ANOTHER VOICE Long live the mother-in-law!

Reaction from LADY LARK. *A ruckus.*

The CHAMBERLAIN *signals the* HERALD, *but* CINDERELLA *indicates that she still wants to speak, and silence falls.*

CINDERELLA Like this, without the bugle. Right now you all think that I'm thinking of these two. But actually I have thought about another person, too, a little person. I am thinking of Cinderella. *(pause: the silence grows in intensity)* That night — oh no, I said "that" because it seems so long ago — I meant "this," tonight, in that room that seemed like the house of the sun, I came to understand lots of things I didn't know. When everyone called me and wanted this and that from me because they thought I was an angel, there was one who didn't want me to touch his viola. Maybe he understood that I wasn't beautiful like all the others thought. For that reason, when I was lost and suffering terribly, and was afraid of the dark, and was even more afraid of the bugles that were looking for me, but also I suffered because I hadn't been obedient, and my clogs came back to me, then he was the only one to recognize me all the same. And he brought me all the way home and then told me "until we meet again," because Cinderella was enough for him. For that reason, even if for a while she was the heavenly angel, she has to go back to being Cinderella. And she thanks Prince Charming with all her heart, but for her, Icarus is good, because his name is Icarus, which seems like the name of a star. Thus Antonia has become princess, and Cinderella marries Icarus. No one has seen him since then, but he is here. He doesn't know that I was the only one who saw him in the middle of everyone. *(She turns to the crowd.)* Icarus, do you want to show yourself?

Movement in the crowd upstage. ICARUS *is found, though no one had realized he was there. He is embarrassed.*

CHAMBERLAIN *(interrogates the* PRINCE *with a look, then proclaims)* Maestro Icarus, the prince would like you to present yourself.

MANY IN THE CROWD *(They push* ICARUS.*)* Go on…. Go, go…

ICARUS *finds himself before the* PRINCE *and lowers his head.*

PRINCE Heaven's will comes to us through the most undreamt-of signs and becomes the prince's will. Icarus and Cinderella,

Cinderella

join hands. *(turns to the court)* Prepare my horse and carriages. *(The* GUARDS *go off to the right.)* And everyone, *(pointing to the people downstage, that is, besides* ANTONIA, *who remains at his side, and* MARINA, LADY LARK, MAESTRO ADEMARO, *the* MEN OF THE COURT*)* everyone to the palace to celebrate the nuptials.

CHAMBERLAIN *(immediately shouting out, he orders the organization of the departure; each of those called gets in place)* Herald! *(the* HERALD *gets in place)* Buglers! *(follow suit)* Their highnesses! *(The* PRINCE *and* ANTONIA *place themselves in the center of the procession)* Lady Cinderella and Maestro Icarus!

CINDERELLA Please, let us be last.

CHAMBERLAIN Then, the family! (LADY LARK *and* MARINA *get in line.)* The Commission! *(The* DIGNITARIES *and* MAESTRO ADEMARO *get in place, and the* CHAMBERLAIN *in front of them.)* To the carriages!

The bugles sound, and the procession moves quickly toward the exit on the right. Applause from the PEOPLE, *who exit behind the court. When the last are disappearing,* CINDERELLA, *hanging on tightly to* ICARUS, *keeps him behind, stops, and turns him toward the* FAIRY GODMOTHER *at the window.*

CINDERELLA Fairy godmother, you're not coming with us?

GODMOTHER The godmother, who is no longer a fairy, is quite content. And she closes the window because the fable is finished. *(She gracefully retreats, closing the window.)*

CINDERELLA *and* ICARUS *look for a moment in silence at the closed window. The bugles are heard, further away. The two join hands and look out, toward the procession. A few seconds of silence. They don't move. The bugles, further away still. Again a few seconds of silence. The episode comes to a close.*

The End

This Book Was Completed on 24 September 2013
at Italica Press, New York. It Is Set in
Adobe Garamond, Luna and
Marlett and Printed on
Acid-Free Paper.

www.ingramcontent.com/pod-product-compliance
Lightning Source LLC
Chambersburg PA
CBHW031144160426
43193CB00008B/248